GREAT IDEAS IN TEACHING HEALTH

Donna Champeau
Oregon State University

Allyn and Bacon
Boston · London · Toronto · Sydney · Tokyo · Singapore

Contents

II.   Health Skills

III.   General Health

IV. Alcohol, Tobacco and Other Drugs

V.   Violence and Abuse

VI. Human Sexuality

VII. Emotional Health

VIII.   HIV Disease/STDS

IX.   Nutrition

Preface

The "art and science" of health education is not any easy element to convey. Skilled educators must use their natural talents as well as the "tools" of the trade in order to be effective in the classroom, in the community, and in other settings where knowledge about health is being presented. Knowing when to use specific tools, how to use specific tools, and which tools would be most effective for specific audiences is often a major challenge for health educators.

Let's face it, not everyone is a "natural" teacher with dynamic interpersonal skills, the ability to "hold" an audience or class, or provide a stimulating environment for learning about health. Also, many of us have difficulties in terms of multiple obligations, not enough time or not enough energy to think of one more "creative" idea for helping our students learn material and apply basic behavioral principles to real life settings. For those of you who are new to the field and don't have a lot of experience in teaching health topics, and those of you who have been around for awhile and are still using yesterday's "worn out" ideas, this book is intended to provide you with the help you are looking for.

Compiled by real health education teachers and tried out in the classrooms of the nation, this set of creative teaching ideas is designed to:

- Provide new and creative methodologies for use in a variety of topical areas.

- Establish a behavioral/theoretical basis for many of the applied exercises/labs that we often use in our classes.

- Establish objective guidelines for using specific tools. Rather than merely doing a class exercise, we have tried to provide clear objectives for use and suggest possible outcomes that you might expect.

- Provide step-by-step procedures for completing the assigned exercises. In some cases, modifications for large/small group utilization has been provided.

- Infuse new techniques and technologies into the health education classroom.

The text itself is divided into nine areas: Promoting Behavioral Changes; Health Skills; General Health; Alcohol, Tobacco and Other Drugs; Violence and Abuse; Human Sexuality; Emotional Health; HIV Disease/STDs; and Nutrition. You may find that some of the teaching ideas can be used in other health areas that you are teaching, as well as in the Personal Health and Wellness areas.

In short, this text is a work in progress. We actively sought ideas from the 1996 cohort of health educators in the field. We synthesized these efforts into a uniform body of work, after carefully selecting the BEST of the submitted ideas. In the future, we will expand upon these ideas and seek your feedback as to how the ideas actually worked. We hope that you find these materials useful. Please let us know if we can be of additional help. Good luck.

ACKNOWLEDGMENTS

I would like to thank Georgia Davis for her time in the formatting of the text in this book and her devoted patience in the attention to detail. I would also like to thank Mary Kriener and Suzy Spivey from Allyn and Bacon for their help and guidance during the planning and editing of the text. Finally, I would like to thank all the health educators that took the time to submit a teaching idea. I believe that their efforts will make a difference.

Perceptions

Submitted by Kristine Brown, Ph.D., HES
Florida Atlantic University, Davie, FL

Communication skills often are overlooked in education. As a result, poor communication skills are abundant in our society and are the underlying cause of conflict in many situations. It is essential to recognize that we all have different perceptions, and our perceptions do not necessarily represent reality. This activity is designed to help students recognize and understand the influence of our perceptions on our ability to communicate effectively.

Objectives

Following completion of the activity, students will be able to:

1. identify barriers to effective communication,

2. identify factors influencing our perceptions, and

3. recognize and understand that everyone perceives things differently.

Materials Needed

paper and pencils

Estimated Time

15 minutes

Description of Activity

1. Begin by asking students to recall the last time that they got into an argument or felt frustrated when talking with someone. Ask for a volunteer to relay his/her experience.

2. Brainstorm a list of barriers to effective communication (differing perceptions).

3. Have students pair up. One person in each pair moves his/her desk so that the back is facing the front of the room. The person with his/her back to the front is the "Receiver" and the person facing the front is the "Sender."

4. Write a noun on the chalkboard or overhead transparency (e.g. car, tree, etc.); the Sender is to describe the word and the Receiver is to draw according to the descriptions given by the sender.

5. The rules are:

   - Receiver cannot speak or use any form of nonverbal communication.

   - Sender must place hands in his/her lap (no body movements).

   - Sender cannot use geometrical shapes in their clues

     (e.g. "draw a circle).

   - Receiver cannot complete the drawing on his/her own if they guess what it is. They must draw exactly as the sender describes.

   - Sender should describe the word using descriptions such as "put your pencil in the center of the page and draw a line about 2 inches long going towards the bottom of the page."

   - Sender cannot say things such as "no, not like that." Receiver draws according to what he/she hears. Sender must continue with descriptions.

6. Give students 3-5 minutes to complete the drawing.

7. Have each pair hold up their drawing and compare with others. Ask Receivers to guess the word (depending on the time available, have students switch roles and repeat activity).

8. Ask why there are no pictures exactly alike and yet the word was the same for everyone (no two people perceive things in the exact same way). Ask which picture is the right picture (there are no right or wrong pictures). Discuss factors that influence our perceptions (attitudes, values, beliefs, past experiences, etc.).

9. Ask both the senders and the receivers to explain their feelings and/or frustrations that they experienced during the activity. Ask how these feelings compare to feelings they have had in other situations (such as the last time they got into an argument).

10. Explain that we will always have different perceptions and that there is no way to make everyone perceive things the same way. Ask how we can avoid and/or deal with conflict that is a result of misperceptions (open communication!).

Evaluation

Have students write a paper and include the following:

1. Briefly describe a situation that resulted in an argument based only your perceptions.

2. Now briefly describe the situation from the viewpoint of the other person.

3. If you could push a "rewind button," what would you do differently? (be specific)

Identifying Health Issues in Your Community

Submitted by Maxine Davis, BS, MA
Eastern Washington University, Cheney, WA
and
Deanna Cooper, BA, MPH
Spokane County Health District, Spokane, WA

Maxine Davis is currently a professor of Health Education at EWU with 33 years of teaching experience in teacher preparation. Deanna Cooper is a Public Health Educator with diverse experience in coalition building and general health education.

Enclosed you will find information on the development of an Adolescent Health Consortium by the Spokane County Health Department. The Health Consortium consisted of over one-hundred health, social service, education, law enforcement, mental health, legislative and media professionals concerned about health problems specific to adolescents. The model used by this group to define local health problems and potential preventive intervention strategies is entitled *Assessment Protocol for Excellence in Public Health* (APEXPH). Several of the steps outlined in this process include identifying direct and indirect contributing factors for health problems, and developing preventive strategies to minimize those contributing factors, thereby reducing the health problem. Maxine took part in this coalition as a representative of the Health Education Program at Eastern Washington University and adapted several of the processes undergone by this group for use at Eastern Washington University. The following teaching strategy, used with Community Health Education seniors, resulted from this adaptation.

Objectives

Through the process of developing the health strategies and programs that were the objectives of the above-mentioned coalition, Maxine recognized the individual needs that each community might have would differ from community to community. She saw a need for young health professionals in undergraduate training to be able to first establish what the health problems were, secondly identify the direct contributing factors for those problems, thirdly identify the indirect contributing factors leading to those health problems, and lastly to develop programs and strategies to meet these needs. She believed that if the student could follow this process as developed by the APEXPH Community Process, which is public domain information, they would learn to pinpoint specific problems germane to their communities and develop appropriate strategies and programs in response.

Materials

Materials needed are the APEXPH flow chart and the students' creativity.

Time

The time needed for the lesson can range from two 50-minute periods to a week, depending on how many health problem areas you wish to explore.

Presentation of the Activity

Several days prior to the lesson, students are asked to think about, inquire, or do some minimal research on what they see as important health issues in their specific community. You can vary this assignment by being more specific by asking the student to identify special needs people, people of color, or people from diverse ethnic backgrounds.

During the actual class assignment, students are grouped according to similarly identified health problems from similar kinds of community demographics. They then brainstorm to identify direct and indirect contributing factors to the health problem. This process usually takes a full 50 minutes with only 2-3 health problem areas being addressed. Thus, there may be a need for perhaps an entire week of class if many health areas are to be explored.

During the second 50-minute period, students develop strategies and programs that might be of value in solving the health problems they identified. In closing the lesson, students refer to the finalized booklet that was developed by the Spokane County Health District Coalition efforts. Students first evaluate how well they thought they developed their strategies and programs. Then, they are asked to review the Spokane County Health Coalition's final report and look for similarities and differences that existed in their community strategies and programs that were developed by local professionals.

This exercise should be used with senior level heath education major students. The student should have some background in analytical thinking processes and most of their major coursework completed. The instructor is not "looking for" right or wrong answers but merely challenging the student to problem-solve.

If any additional information is needed on this health education strategy, please contact Maxine Davis at (509) 359-2872 or Deanna Cooper at (509) 324-1473.

An Autobiography or an Obituary?
Submitted by John S. Carter, Ph.D.
The Citadel, Charleston, SC

Teachers need to personalize and individualize health courses. Each student brings his/her own upbringing, experiences, hopes, and fears into every classroom. A teacher's responsibility is to somehow help each student to learn how to ask the right questions and find the best possible answers.

Lesson Objectives

Upon completion of this lesson the student should be able to:

1. understand/learn that each has a myriad of choices when it comes to personal health habits and behaviors;

2. examine introspectively the opportunities he/she has;

3. more readily accept self-responsibility for one's actions;

4. present themselves as a real "individual person" to the instructor, not just an ID number or a face/body occupying a classroom desk,; and

5. enhance written and oral communication skills.

Materials Required

The assignment is to write a 1-2 page paper using appropriate citations as required.

Time Allocations

This project should be assigned no less than two weeks prior to the due date.

How to Present the Lesson

Write a 1-2 page paper describing who you are, or who you would like to become or be remembered as. An autobiography and/or an obituary assignment is encouraged. Include information, feelings, and self-perceptions about one's hometown, family, friends, accomplishments, awards, interests, hobbies, career goals, plans for the future, and concerns.

Evaluation Techniques

Aside from grading papers on content and mechanics, teachers should encourage students to read selected passages. Teachers should direct classroom discussions to address solutions to "global" problems mentioned in assignments.

Help Your Public Health Department Solve Real Problems

Submitted by John S. Carter, Ph.D.
The Citadel, Charleston, SC

Students need to know that every day a myriad of real-world health problems occur to people living in a community. Furthermore, the Public Health Service and its personnel usually have more people with health problems than they can adequately provide.

Lesson Objectives

Upon completion of this lesson the student should be able to:

1. help solve real health problems by collecting, consolidating, analyzing, and disseminating data;

2. construct depictions (tables, charts, graphs, maps) of data collected;

3. gain professional and career direction which may lead to futures in the public and/or private health care industry;

4. help establish collegial relationships between the college/university, public health personnel, and the community;

5. enhance written and oral communication skills; and

6. adopt the decision-making, problem-solving model.

Materials Required

Students should maintain a daily logbook of "work" experiences, noting what they (a) accomplished and (b) learned. Class participants will choose a client- or community-health problem encountered during the "internship." Analyze the problem using the decision-making model; offer at least three alternative solutions, consequences of each, and estimated costs or savings (if any).

Time Allocations

This concept is best assigned for an entire grading period extending over several weeks or months.

How to Present the Lesson

Organization of Class   Students can act as public health "Investigators" conducting field work involving health issues, ie. seat belt and car seat restraints, bicycle and motorcycle helmet practices; data collection/compilation and construction of maps may also be needed. Other options include working with WIC programs and public sanitarians/restaurant inspectors.

Variations for Different Populations

For individuals interested in research, clinical work, health education, and/or field studies, the U.S. Public Health Service is an excellent introductory "proving ground."

Evaluation Techniques

In addition to grading written work for content and mechanics, opportunities for in-class presentations of case studies or projects should be provided. On-site visits from college/university faculty to student "interns" is encouraged. Feedback from Public Health personnel who

Think About Learning Through Relationships

Submitted by Lucy Stroble, Ed.D.
University of Maine at Presque Isle, Presque Isle, ME

Whether same sex or opposite sex, the peer relationships of a college student are of primary importance at this developmental stage. The breakup of a romance or friendship or loneliness for high school friends shakes the self-confidence of a student and causes depression and anxiety. Helping students to think about all of the relationships in their lives, what they contribute to each relationship, and what they learn from relationships can bolster their self-confidence and improve social skills.

The objective of this activity is 1) to stimulate students to think about all of their past, present, and even future relationships, 2) make a positive value statement about those relationships, and 3) determine what their relationships have taught them or how they have taught others. This activity encourages students to become analytical and philosophical about life events. The activity can be used to stimulate discussion and bond a group that is already somewhat familiar with one another. This can be used as a "hot seat" activity, in small groups, or in a large group.

Procedures

Introduce the students to the stated objectives. Tell students that while the questions are probing and thought-provoking, they are not intended to be intimidating or embarrassing. Remind them that they may pass or ask for another question.

Write all of the questions on 3 x 5 cards. For the hot seat activity, put a seat in front of the room, facing the class. The instructor may lead the activity, ask for an activity leader, or rotate discussion leaders. Ask for a volunteer to come and sit in the chair and choose a question. Ask the person to read the question or the activity leader may read it to them. They may answer it, pass, or allow a member of the class to answer it. A general discussion of the question by the whole class may ensue. When finished, the person picks another group member to sit in the hot seat. To insure full group participation, make sure everyone answers a question either in the hot seat or in the audience. Questions may be repeated if necessary or desirable.

If used in small groups, give each group a question and ask group members to respond verbally or in writing. If used as a large group activity, ask students to silently generate an answer, then have a group discussion. The element of spontaneity enhances the effectiveness of this activity.

When the activity is finished, ask students to write a paragraph describing what they learned as a result of this activity. Writing prompts may include:

"One thing I have learned through my relationships with others is..."

"A person can learn about himself/herself through relationships with others." Write a paragraph agreeing or disagreeing with this statement using examples to support your argument.

This is a versatile activity and can be used with any content area and most adult age groups. The idea of learning from a relationship is a twist on the usual relationship activities and discussions. It is especially useful for health education majors engaged in exploring diverse learning styles and other more formal pedagogical issues.

Think About Learning Through Relationships

* Who do you anticipate that you will learn from in the future?

*Talk about something a grandparent taught you.

*Talk about something you've learned from a non-romantic relationship with a person of the opposite sex.

*Talk about something you've learned from a relationship with a person of another race or culture.

*What have you learned about life and people through a pet?

*What have you learned from a person with a handicap?

*Talk about a poor teacher who taught you something valuable.

*Talk about something you think another person has learned from you as a result of being related or in a relationship with you.

*What has a romantic relationship taught you about yourself?

*What have you learned through the death of someone close?

*Tell us about something you learned from a sibling.

*Talk about a relationship that was affected by the use of alcohol or other drugs.

*Tell us about something you learned from a childhood friendship.

*Think about a romance that ended. What did you learn from that ending?

*What is the first thing you remember learning as a very young child? From whom did you learn it?

*Tell us about a skill that you learned from someone other than your parent or a teacher.

*What skill have you taught someone else?

* If you are a parent, what have your children taught you?

* If you are not a parent, what do you think you have taught your parents?

*Besides this class, what is the most recent thing that you have learned from another person?

6

Investigating Behavior Change at Multiple Levels

Submitted by Suzanne E. Teall, Ph.D.
Montana State University, Bozeman, MT

There are multiple views on the causes of and solutions to the burden of disease in this country. Some believe that individuals cause their own disease, therefore, solutions lie in individual behavior change. Some believe that disease causation occurs at a macro level and behavior change should occur at the system level through policy change. An integrated view also exists. This view is that healthy behavior change occurs through a combination of individual and policy-level efforts. This lesson addresses the pros and cons of thinking and working on behavior change strategies at individual, policy and multiple levels.

Objectives

1. Learners will be able to distinguish between individual and policy-level behavior change strategies.

2. Learners will be able to compare and contrast the pros and cons of behavior change strategies at the individualand policy levels.

3. Learners will be able to synthesize positive and negative aspects of individual and policy-level behavior change strategies from varying viewpoints.

Materials

Documents that discuss the history, advantages and disadvantages of behavior change at individual and policy levels. Placards with the following printed in large letters: senior citizens, physicians, school board members, college students, members of house of representatives, residents of public housing, managers of health insurance companies, homeless individuals, adolescents, business executives.

Examples of Articles

Individual: Stachnik, T., Stoffelmayr, B., & Hoppe, R. B. (1983). "Prevention, behavior change, and chronic disease." In T. G. Burish & L.A. Bradley, (Eds.), *Coping with chronic disease: Research and Applications* (pp. 447-473). New York: Academic Press.

Policy: Schmidt, T. L., Pratt, M. & Howze, E. (1995). "Policy as intervention: Environmental and policy approaches to the prevention of cardiovascular disease." *American Journal of Public Health*, 85(9), 1207-121 1.

Time Needed

Two 50-minute class sessions.

Activity

Session 1:　　Have learners read documents on behavior change strategies at the individual and policy level. Divide class into groups of 3-4 students per group. Each group will represent a different constituency from among the following: senior citizens, physicians, school board members, college students at your university, individuals from house of representatives in your region, individuals living in public housing in your community, managers of health insurance companies, adolescents, homeless individuals, and executives at a corporation in your community. Each group is to: 1) discuss the pros and cons of behavior change strategies at individual and policy levels from the perspective of their group; and 2) devise solutions to reduce the burden of disease in their community using this perspective.

Session 2:　　Arrange room so that groups from the first session are sitting together. Place placards that state the group name on the table or desk. Announce to the class that you are holding a town meeting to start the discussion on what should be done to decrease the burden of disease and disability in the community. State that they have been brought together to devise strategies that will represent the different voices in the community. Discuss the ground rules: I) students are to stay in character of the group they belong to; 2) there should be no attacks on individuals; and 3) critique but do not criticize ideas and opinions of other groups and individuals. Begin the town meeting with one group. Have them present their solutions of effective healthy behavior change. Allow other groups to ask questions, comment, critique and offer their views. Continue discussion until all groups have shared their strategies. End with a discussion on differences and similarities among groups and what, if any, behavior change strategies could be realized that would satisfy all groups.

Variations

Depending on class size, fewer or more groups can be formed.

Evaluation

Learners can be evaluated on input into the discussion or by quiz or test questions assessing history, pros and cons of behavior change strategies at the individual and policy level.

7

Disease Mnemonics:
A Learner-Centered Activity
Submitted by Dr. Helen M. Welle and
Dr. Michael J. Ludwig
Georgia Southern University, Statesboro, GA

Health promotion/disease prevention strategies need to be creative, flexible, and interactive to reach teenagers and young adults. This teaching technique provides an opportunity for this audience to link health promotion/disease prevention strategies with personal experiences and enables them to incorporate these principles into their lifestyles. Students will work collectively to formulate a mnemonic device to aid in the retention of information concerning diseases and the disease process. That information will be used to generate prevention principles related to disease prevention. The activity also enables students to practice social skills, decision-making skills, and presentation skills.

Educational Objectives

1. Students will summarize key components of various diseases using a supplied list of characteristics.

2. Students will synthesize a mnemonic device to aid in the retention of information concerning diseases and the disease process.

3. Students will present their mnemonic device to the class.

4. Students will generate disease prevention strategies based on information gleaned from the presentations.

Intended Audience   High School and College (adaptable to any age group and health content area).

Materials

For this activity, the students will need available to them: (1) information about the disease (pamphlets or health textbook), (2) poster board and markers or transparencies and overhead markers, (3) overhead projector, (4) handouts with examples, and (5) creative mindset.

Time

Total time estimation is a minimum of 50 minutes, assuming 5 groups are used and presentations are kept to five minutes each. The instructor may choose to let this activity run longer, if needed.

Methods and Content.

The focus of this activity is to enable students to learn about various diseases and the components of these diseases. Through cooperative action in small groups (4 to 5 students each), students will decide which key characteristics are to be included in their description of a specific disease. Each disease is broken down into disease name (formal and informal), identification (notable distinguishing characteristics), agent, incubation, transmission, symptoms, treatment, and prevention. Each mnemonic device will include all eight (8) components listed above. It is the students' decision, as a result of reading the literature and consulting with their peers, which specific elements will be included in each of the 8 categories. Examples of mnemonic devices will be presented by the instructor. Once the elements of the disease are decided, students will use the first letter of each element to devise a creative mnemonic phrase. This mnemonic is put on a poster board or overhead transparency and presented to the class.

Evaluation Technique/Closure

Successful completion and presentation of the mnemonic device is used to evaluate this lesson. Students will be asked to formulate general prevention principles after listening to each of their peers' presentations.

Table 1. Mnemonic Example for Tetanus.

Disease Characteristic	Elements	Mnemonic Device
Name	Staphylococcal Food Poisoning	Steve
Identification	Food with Staph toxins undercooked meat	Fed
Agent	Staphylococcus Aureus	Sarah
Incubation	Two to four hours	Tainted
Transmission	Pork, beef	Porkchops
Symptoms diarrhea	Nausea, vomiting,	Nausea
Treatment	Oral rehydration, IV fluid replacement therapy	Overtook
Prevention	Proper cooling and heating procedures	People

Table 2. Mnemonic Exampled for Gonorrhea

Disease Characteristic	Elements	Mnemonic Device
Name	Gonorrhea, "Clap"	Gooey
Identification	Second (2nd) most common STD	Slop
Agent	Gonococcus	Gives
Incubation	Two (2) to (7) day	The
Transmission	Body fluids, sexual activit	Body
Symptoms	Asymptomatic, painful urination	Awful
Treatment	Antibiotics	Aching
Prevention	Protected sex, Abstinence	Parts

8

Analyze a Health Decision
Submitted by John S. Carter, Ph.D.
The Citadel, Charleston, SC

Many personal decisions are poor ones because consequences of one's actions are rarely considered. Conversely, good decisions are generally due to careful weighing of alternatives and contemplation of what may happen if each choice was pursued.

Lesson Objectives

Upon completion of this lesson the student should be able to:

1. examine why good/poor health decisions are made,

2. consider the importance of considering the consequences of one's behavior,

3. adopt the decision-making/problem-solving model, and

4. read, think, self-reflect, problem-solve, and write more effectively.

Materials Required

The assignment is to write a 1-2 page paper using appropriate citations as required.

Time Allocations

This project should be assigned no less than two weeks prior to the due date.

How to Present the Lesson

Give class members two weeks to locate a current event (newspaper, magazine, TV news) in which an individual's good or bad health decision resulted in either positive or negative outcomes.
Students are asked to develop a four-paragraph paper based on this current event.

The first paragraph describes the event. The second paragraph identifies "cues" or "triggers" to the event (in the absence of all specific details, students should speculate as to what may have happened in the hours, days, weeks, or years preceding the event). The third paragraph discusses historical steps or precursors which may have led the party (ies) to the triggering stage (what situations or conditions could have led to the final decision). The fourth paragraph is the writer's advice to the victims or parties, had they sought his/her advice, in order to resolve the problem.

Evaluation Techniques

Aside from grading papers on content and mechanics, the teacher can orchestrate class discussions of several events. Questions such as ,"What can be derived from studying these various events?"; "How could negative consequences have been minimized?" ; "What positive behaviors/habits would have been preferable?", "What alternative solutions can you offer?" can begin class discussions.

Credits: *This activity idea came from an article in the* Joumal of Health Education *in approximately 1993-1994. This is a publication of the Association for the Advancement of Health Education, part of the American Alliance for Health, Physical Education, Recreation and Dance.*

9

Personal Health Journal

Submitted ay Jane A. Petrillo, Ed.D.
Northern Kentucky University, Highland Heights, KY

This activity is very broad and can be related and linked to the many content areas covered in a Personal Health course in addition to drawing upon the student's interests and experiences. My teaching activity is that of a Personal Health Journal which is a primary and essential requirement of the course. As we know, a journal is a combination of diary and class notebook which reflects and records the student's private thoughts and experiences in relation to academic content. Journals can serve as a valuable tool in literary, verbal, and cognitive development. Journal writing is a practical and useful approach to enhancing student's knowledge, understanding, and application of subject matter and in the development of critical thinking skills.

Objectives

(Refer to Forms A and B)

The Personal Health Journal is a requirement of the course and begins on the second week of class (Quarter or Semester) and is due at the conclusion of the Quarter or Semester. The Personal Health Journal has four primary objectives which are identified as sections one through four. Objective/Section I includes the Behavior Change Section. This first section requires the completion of a Health Behavior Questionnaire, a Behavior Intervention Form, a Behavior Change Contract, and the daily recording of health behaviors specific to the adherence or non-adherence of the Behavior Change Program. Objective/Section II requires fifteen (one page) reflections on class content, discussions, readings, materials, and videos which must include personal reflection of that content specific to the student's life, knowledge, and experiences. Objective/Section III includes ten (one page) entries which are summaries of current issues and topics related to Personal Health found from any media source, journal, etc. A full reference is required at the top of each summary page. Objective/Section IV requires the completion of numerous activities (either found in Access to Health textbook or provided by the instructor) which provide for direct reflection, clarification, and application of lesson content and concepts. (Instructor materials required in this section under Class Activities will be provided upon request).

Presentation Of the Activity

The Personal Health Journal requirements are reviewed and discussed on the first day of class at the beginning of the Semester during the review of the course syllabus. On the second class meeting, student's complete the Health Behavior Questionnaire and the instructor reviews the Personal Health Journal Activities once again. The following week, the students must identify one health behavior to be changed or maintained throughout the semester and share their behavior change goal with the class. After lecture and discussion on factors influencing behavior and the various behavior theories (Chapters one and two), students complete the Behavior Intervention Form (Refer to Form C) and the Behavior Change Contract (Refer to Form D). After this point, the instructor reviews student's progress, or lack of, on the Behavior Change Program and any other Journal activities with the class periodically throughout the semester. The Journal activities are primarily completed on the student's time rather than class time. The exception to this case is when a class activity (Recorded in the Class Activities Section in Journal) is conducted during the lesson.

Evaluation of Personal Health Journal

Journals are awarded points for entries yet composition errors should not be considered. Written language in the form of journal entries is a means for the instructor to learn about and evaluate the student's understanding of subject matter, concerns, and experiences in addition to their writing abilities. It is imperative that instructor's maintain complete confidentiality in the reading, review, and evaluation of Journal content. The total value of the Journal is 100 Points. Section I accounts for 20 Points, Section II is worth 30 Points, Section III is worth 10 Points, and Section IV is worth a total of 40 Points.

Conclusion

The criteria, requirements, activities, entries, and point value of the Personal Health Journal is certainly dependent upon the instructor and the objectives of the course. I have provided one approach to developing and enhancing student's knowledge, thinking skills, writing skills, and application of content in a Personal Health Course. I am hopeful that you find this activity useful in a Personal Health Supplementary Reader.

BEHAVIORAL INTERVENTION FORM

1.   STATE BEHAVIOR TO BE CHANGED/MAINTAINED.

2.   REASONS FOR CHANGING/MAINTAINING THIS
      BEHAVIOR.

      A.

      B.

      C.

      D.

      E.

3.   IDENTIFY YOUR CURRENT BASELINE FOR THIS
      BEHAVIOR.

4.   STATE BEHAVIOR CHANGE IN THE FORM OF A PRECISE
      BEHAVIORAL GOAL/OBJECTIVE.

5.   DESCRIBE SHORT TERM REWARD AND/OR
      CONTINGENCIES.

      A.

      B.

      C.

      D.

      E

6.   DESCRIBE INTERMEDIATE AND LONG-TERM REWARDS
     AND/OR CONTINGENCIES.

    A.

    B.

    C.

    D.

    E.

7.   LIST THE POSITIVE AND THE'NEGATIVE FORCES THAT
     WILL HELP YOU CHANGE OR MAINTAIN THE
     BEHAVIOR.

    POSITIVE   NEGATIVE

8.   DEVISE A RECORD-KEEPING SYSTEM APPROPRIATE
     FOR YOUR INTERVENTION AND ATTACH IT TO THIS
     FORM.

9.   COMPLETE THE BEHAVIOR CHANGE CONTRACT AND
     ATTACH IT TO THIS FORM.

Form D

BEHAVIOR CHANGE/MAINTENANCE CONTRACT

I_____

AGREE TO:_____

_____

FOR THE PERIOD FROM_____TO_____

IF I PERFORM THE BEHAVIOR, I WILL REWARD MYSELF AS
FOLLOWS:

_____

IF I DO NOT PERFORM THE ABOVE BEHAVIOR, I AGREE TO
FOREGO THE ABOVE REWARDS

SIGNED:_____DATE:_____
WITNESS #1:_____DATE:_____
WITNESS #2:_____ DATE:_____
WITNESS #3:_____ DATE:_____

10

He Said, She Said...Gender Communication

Submitted by Shelley Hamill, M. Ed.
Livngstone College, Salisbury, NC

In today's society, communication is critical for success. Corporations, industries, governments, educators and countless others rely on various modes of telecommunication to keep apprised of current demands, issues, needs and trends. Yet on a more personal day-to-day level, individuals have a difficult time communicating in a one-on-one, face-to-face situation.

Without clear and honest communication, many misconceptions or misinterpretations occur. The area where this is most evident is male/female relationships.

Many articles have been written in earnest and jest trying to decipher what a man means when he says something compared to what a woman means when she says the same thing. The recommendations are always the same; talk with each other: listen to each other, and try to understand each other.

Health educators have a prime opportunity to keep the lines open between the sexes by facilitating honest, non-threatening conversations to help everyone understand the roles we play and perhaps why we act as we do. The following activity has been used successfully at the collegiate level and could easily be used in grades 6 and above to facilitate positive dialogue between the sexes.

Objective

Participants will be able to sustain a positive group dialogue that fosters greater understanding between the sexes.

Materials

Two circles of chairs, blackboard or overhead with questions, paper and pencil for the recorder in each group. (The circles should be as far apart as possible so that the groups will not listen to each other. If possible, move one group into the hallway for their discussion.)

Procedure

Divide the class into male and female groups, each to the assigned circle. A recorder is designated. It should be emphasized that this activity is about understanding one another and that we should be honest in our responses. Once everyone is in place, two questions are asked.

1. What is it you least understand about the opposite sex?
2. What is it you most wish the opposite sex understood about you?

Each group is to generate 8 to 10 responses to each question. (If you have arranged for a group to be out of the room, split them, go over the questions and then send them out). Once the lists have been generated, ask the groups to then cull them down to their top five responses for each question. When the group work is complete, bring the class back together. Toss a coin to decide which group goes first. For example, the male group wins the toss and elects to list their responses first. The recorder for that group should list and explain their top five responses to question #1. The leader must be very firm that there will be no verbal assaults, that no one will be allowed to speak without raising his/her hand and that the items listed may be general impressions and may not pertain to them specifically. Having seen the responses, the female group is then asked to select three items they would like to address. They may ask for clarification as needed on the meaning of any item. Anyone within the female group may address the issues one at a time, without interruption from the male group, by raising her hand. After the first item has been addressed by all of the females who wish to respond , one person from the male group may respond. The females then proceed to the next item following the same format.

Having completed the first listing, it is now time for the females to list their responses and to follow the same procedures as before. Again, remind students of the rules for responding. After both groups have processed question one, process the second question, but have the group who lost the coin toss go first.

You may conclude the activity by processing some of the following questions:

1. Were the males and females in this class really speaking and listening carefully to each other? Examples? How does this affect the success of a relationship?

2. Did some issues seem to create hostility? Which ones? Why do you think they created strong feelings?

3. How is forming opinions based on hearsay, stereotypes and misinterpretations destructive in a relationship?

4. What happens if you make assumptions because a person is male or female without checking it out with them?

This entire activity takes about an hour. The small group activity and their exchanges can be done in ten minutes. If you do not have time to process all of these questions in class, assign them as journal entry questions and give students a handout with the questions listed.

Evaluation

Pass out a notecard to each person. Ask them to write 4 words. "Today I learned that...". Give them 3-5 minutes for responses. Take them up as students leave. Read some at the beginning of the next class as a review.

Communicating Effectively: Multi-Media Metaphors

Submitted by Carol Plugge, Ph.D.
Lamar University, Beaumont, TX

Communication is said to be the key to successful relationships and lack of communication to be the demise. Communication has many different definitions, but can be simply defined as a transformational exchange process in which meanings are created and interpreted with symbols during human interaction. Communication is dependent on human interaction and interpretation of symbols. Individuals draw on past experience, thoughts, and attitudes to determine the meaning of the communicated symbols. If the individuals have different past experiences, then confusion of the meaning of symbols can cause poor understanding during the communication process.

Individual differences in interpretation of communicated symbols can be a function of many components including, but not limited to, culture, gender, geographic area, ethnic background, home setting, educational level, and physical challenges.

Because human beings are extremely dynamic and have individualized backgrounds, it can be helpful to transform symbols into common, standardized levels in order to enhance understanding.

Metaphors are excellent conduits for creating a standard level of interpretation. By simplifying a concept to be communicated into more common terms that most everyone can understand, the possible interpretations become limited and understanding tends to become crystal clear. Metaphors can be simple, such as describing exhaustion as, "I'm dog tired," to describing a complex relationship problem as, "I feel like a dog when you bark commands at me."

The lesson can be expanded by including a multimedia component. Information is more meaningful and better retained when students are actively involved in the learning process. Multimedia supplies (clay, construction paper, feathers, paper clips, pipe cleaners, magazines, paints, markers, etc.) can be utilized to enhance the learning process by allowing the student to build a multimedia model of his/her metaphor. Through the construction of the model the student can better explain and remember the symbolic meaning of the chosen metaphor.

Objectives

By the end of this lesson, student will be able to:

1. define communication,
2. discuss the importance of symbols in communication,
3. define metaphor,
4. list at least three examples of metaphors,
5. write a personal metaphor based on a feeling or conversational topic, and
6. construct a personal metaphor from multi media supplies.

Materials

1. Brief introduction to the concepts of communication and metaphors.
2. Chalk board or butcher paper and marker.
3. Examples of simple metaphors.
4. Multimedia supplies such as clay, construction paper, markers, colors, pipe cleaners, scissors, glue, feathers, string, yarn, paper clips, etc. - project can be completed with just a few supplies or many depending on availability.
5. 12" x 12" pieces of cardboard for a base.

Time

This lesson will take approximately 60 minutes depending on the age of the participants. It usually takes a little longer with older individuals, due to more interaction and discussion.

Description

This lesson can be used with individuals of all ages. The depth of the discussion on communication and metaphors will depend on the maturity of the individuals and their abstract thinking capabilities. This lesson is most likely appropriate for student age 12 through adult because abstract thinking skills are necessary for understanding the concepts of symbols and metaphors. The lesson can be adapted either for adults, by increasing the depth of the discussion on communication and metaphors and sharing the meanings of the models, or for adolescents by somewhat simplifying the concepts and allowing individuals to proceed at their own pace.

(5minutes) Open class session with a game. Instruct the students to form groups according to their favorite color. Then have them group by the month they were born, without talking to each other. Briefly discuss verbal versus nonverbal forms of communication and which is easier to use.

(**15 minutes**) Introduce the concept of communication. Ask the students to brainstorm the meaning of communication and form a definition from their brainstormed ideas - or introduce your own definition. Communication is a transformational exchange process in which meanings are created and interpreted with symbols during human interaction, to provide information exchange through written, spoken, or behavioral symbols. A method of giving information to another individual, etc.. Come up with your own definition of communication.

Discuss the importance of communication in our world, society, community, school, home, and relationships, and what problems can arise with lack of communication or miscommunication. Discuss the connection between communication and symbolism and how communication is a string of symbols that may be interpreted differently by different individuals.

Introduce the concept of metaphors and how they can be word pictures or explanations for the symbols we use in communication. Give the students a couple of examples of simple metaphors such as: He is as sharp as a tack, Life is like a bowl of cherries, I am as happy as a lark, I feel like the invisible man, It's raining cats and dogs, and then have the students continue to brainstorm more examples of feelings or topics of conversation.

(**10 minutes**) Have the students privately think of a feeling or a topic of conversation the would like to communicate to another individual. Have them write down their feeling or topic and then think of a metaphor that would help to describe the feeling or topic. Remind them that the metaphor will help to explain the symbol being communicated. Adults may want to a choose a metaphor that uses word pictures related to a topic of interest for the person they are trying to communicate to. Example: If a woman is trying to describe her feelings in a relationship and her husband enjoys hunting, she might try to use a hunting metaphor to get his attention such as: I feel that our relationship is like an old rifle that you have thrown to the side because you don't think it works very well anymore. I wish you would take the time to give our relationship some tender loving care like you give your rifles when you want them to keep working properly. The teacher should move about the room and offer help to any students having difficulty with the abstract concepts.

37

Students that are having difficulty may want to choose a simple emotion such as happiness or anger to communicate.

(**15 minutes**) The students will construct a multimedia model of their chosen metaphor. They can use the 12 x 12 pieces of cardboard for a base in which to construct their model. Inform students they have 15 minutes to use any of the supplies they want to visually describe their metaphor and that they will be sharing it with the class.

(**15 minutes**) Ask the students to share their topic or feeling metaphor and explain their model to the class.

End the session by recapping the importance of communication in relationships and the effectiveness of using word pictures/metaphors to help comprehension of the information being communicated.

Evaluation

The evaluation of this session can be objective based and/or qualitative. A pre/post test can be given to assess the ability to achieve the objectives stated. Qualitatively the student can be asked to state their opinions, verbally or written, about the effectiveness of the session and any praise or criticism. I prefer using a combination of qualitative and quantitative evaluation techniques.

12

Teaching Critical Thinking Through The Mock Trial

Submitted by Alice Randolph-Prince, Ph.D.
Southern Illinois University at Edwardsville, IL

Today's teachers must educate children who grow up in front of a television set, who own their own radio, stereo, or computer, and who have access to magazines, libraries, and community education classes. Children are bombarded with some accurate, some biased, and some erroneous information about drug use, nutrition, fitness, and sexual issues that could involve life and death decisions. Students already have formed opinions about health behavior through the media and bring these preconceived notions with them to class. It is sometimes difficult for a student to accept information presented by an instructor, due to conflicting reports on health-related information from the media. In the mock trial technique, information from a variety of sources is analyzed and its validity is "debated." The technique works best with grades 11 through college.

Because health-related issues have a significant impact on values and moral decisions, the mock courtroom trial effectively stimulates critical thinking. Not only does the trial present several aspects of an issue, it offers students opportunities to study various opinions and facts from different perspectives without the teacher being the primary information giver. Thus, students have an opportunity to prepare the trial by analyzing media information and assimilating values and ideas of their peer group, which makes the learning more receptive and meaningful.

Procedures

About two or three weeks before the trial date, the instructor introduces the technique by giving the class examples of possible topics that would lend themselves to a trial format: Should drug testing be done? Should punishments be more severe for drunk drivers? Should harmful weightloss products be promoted by the media? Should fitness facilities be accountable for accurate information and training techniques? Should pregnant women who use drugs be held responsible by the courts for damage done to the unborn child? Should fathers have any rights concerning abortion? Who should be responsible for sexuality education—parents or teachers?

Students are encouraged to brainstorm as many ideas as possible for 20 minutes. All possibilities are discussed to determine if sufficient controversy exists within the group to make the topic arguable; topics then are voted on by the class. After a topic is selected, the instructor develops a scenario, a brief summary of the pros and cons of the issues, indicating arguments for the prosecution and defense, complete with witness assignments (Figure 1).

Every class member receives a handout of the scenario and an opportunity to "volunteer" for the positions of judge, attorneys, and witnesses for both sides. By using two attorneys for each side, students can lend support to each other. The remaining students comprise the jury. It is helpful to ask students if they know how a trial is conducted and give them information concerning trial procedures.

On their own and according to their role in the trial, students research current and accurate information from journals, the U.S. Constitution, textbooks, and lay publications. Twice, prior to the trial date, witnesses meet with their attorneys during the last
10-15 minutes of class to discuss information and strategies. The trial could be held during one class period or the prosecution could present one day and the defense another, depending on the length of the class period.

On the trial date, props such as robe and gavel are available and the classroom is arranged to resemble a courtroom. The bailiff (teacher appointed) starts the trial by calling the court in session. The judge, attorneys, and witnesses proceed to try the case before the jury. After all testimony has been heard and closing arguments presented, the jury leaves the room and debates the information. The jury leaves the room to discuss the decision to protect privacy of opinion as in a real courtroom trial.

After reaching a decision (usually not unanimous due to time constraints), it is presented to the judge by the jury foreman and, time permitting, a class discussion follows of how the
decision was reached. At this time, the teacher points out strengths and weaknesses of the arguments and testimony and identifies controversial aspects concerned with making choices. Students participate in the discussion and add their ideas about the testimony and thrust of the questioning.

Evaluation

The class discussion and trial itself are methods for evaluating student learning. However, the teacher also can assign a reaction paper. Choices can include the pros and cons of the issue, three points students learned from the trial; what students would change about the trial process; or discussion of other issues students hoped to hear debated which came out during the trial process. Another way to partially evaluate the learning process is to remind the class how they voted on the topic when it was originally chosen and count the pro and con votes after the trial ends.

Conclusion

The mock trial works because it is student generated, helps to clarify the values and morals behind the health issues and, most importantly, develops critical thinking skills. While students are researching information for the trial they are demonstrating knowledge about that field. For some teachers, this process may be an acceptable alternative to the traditional research paper or individual report. The trial has been successful at the graduate and undergraduate levels in a variety of health courses. Students also have chosen this method for their presentations in classes outside health education.

Figure 1
Mock Trial Scenario

More and more information about the threat to babies' lives — addiction, life threatening diseases, and deformities — as a result of their mothers' drug use while pregnant is being released to the public. This reality is frightening and deserves examination. The issue on trial is to determine whether or not a woman can be charged with a criminal act if she uses drugs while pregnant.

Points to consider:
1. Some women may not realize that they are pregnant when they use drugs
2. Is the court system capable of making decisions regarding procreation?
3. How far can the justice system go in determining right and wrong?
4. If the mother is not responsible for the child's life, who is?

Prosecution
(Wants to make the mother liable)

Witnesses
1) Physician
2) Right to Life representative

3) Social Worker
4) Your choice

Defense
(Does not believe that in all cases the mother is liable)

Witnesses
1) Nurse
2) Civil
Rights expert
3) Psychiatrist
4) Your choice

13

Listening Skills
Submitted by Cathie Stivers, Ph.D., CHES
Longwood College, Farmville, VA

A popular movie in the 1970s proclaimed that "love means never having to say you're sorry." On the contrary, love means *constantly* having to say "I'm sorry," as well as "I feel like....... I love you," "It upsets me when....... I don't understand," "Am I making sense?," "It's my perception that . . .," "I need . . .," "I want . . . " and "Can we talk?" to give just a few examples. The importance of effective communication in intimate relationships cannot be understated. Aside from talk about sex, the relationship revolves around personal communication about each other's feelings, fears, hopes, dreams, and needs. The quality of the relationship is in fact dependent upon such communication. Unfortunately this type of communication is often taken for granted, with the assumption that "If you love me then you'll know me, and I won't have to say it."

The following is an activity which focuses on the importance of just one component of effective communication: listening. The results will show that listening is not as easy as it seems.

Objectives

At the conclusion of this activity, the student will:

1. discover that human error in listening can distort the true meaning of someone's spoken communication, and

2. be able to describe listening skills necessary for effective communication.

Materials Needed

Four sheets of blank paper; and a pen or pencil.

Time needed

Approximately 30 minutes

Activity

"I Heard it Through the Grapevine"

Divide the class into two evenly-sized groups. (If the class size is fifteen or less, use the whole class as one group.) The class instructor writes a one-sentence message on one sheet of paper, and a different one-sentence message on another sheet. The instructor then whispers one of the messages into the ear of one student in one of the groups. That student, without writing it down or hearing it repeated, whispers what s/he heard to the next group member, and so on until the last group member receives the message. This last person writes the message s/he heard on one of the sheets of paper. The same procedure is followed for the other group with a different message. The instructor then shares with the class the comparisons of the original messages with the final messages reported by each group.

For more interesting results, make one message objective and the other subjective, and compare which of the groups is closer to producing the original message. For example, when this method was used in a college-level personal health class of 32 students, the instructor had a hunch that the more objective or factual message would be remembered better and translated more accurately than the subjective, affective message. Because such a difference has direct implications for interpersonal communication, the instructor sought to determine if a difference did exist.

The results did suggest that the instructor's hunch was true. When the instructor's objective message was "I didn't have enough money with me when I got to the grocery store, so all I could get was milk, bread, and cat food," sixteen students later it became "I wanted to buy some drugs, but I wanted something to eat, so I bought some eggs." The instructor's subjective message, "Whenever I see someone suffering, I feel like I understand their pain, even if I don't know them" became "Something is somewhere and someone doesn't know where that something is."
The activity should conclude with a discussion on the components of effective communication, with an emphasis on listening skills: asking the person to clarify what s/he just said and/or restating what you think s/he said; letting the person know if you don't understand what they're communicating, providing leading questions or statements when the other person is having difficulty communicating and supporting that person if they are having difficulty; affirming what the other person says via verbal or nonverbal communication; allowing for ample reflection time for each to consider what the other has said; and summarizing or bringing closure to the conversation which is satisfactory to both parties (Turner and Rubinson, 1993). If more time is available, the instructor can extend the discussion to cover additional subtopics of communication, such as verbal vs. nonverbal communication and conflict resolution.

Evaluation

The first objective can be measured through the instructor's observation of students' reactions during and after the message relay. The second objective can be measured on a written test, or through students' ability to use what they know during role playing.

14

Using Debate to Develop Health Literacy
Submitted by Mark A. Temple, Ph.D., CHES
Texas Tech University, Lubbock, TX

A health literate student is a creative thinker and problem solver. This student is also self-directed and possesses effective communication skills. I have found debate a useful tool for developing health literate students. Debate helps the student analyze issues, formulate positions, and communicate his or her ideas in a comprehensible fashion. These skills will benefit the student throughout his or her life.

Objectives

1. The learner will analyze data and sources of information.
2. The learner will synthesize material from various sources.
3. The learner will construct supporting and opposing arguments.
4. The learner will present a concise and direct debate.
5. The learner will demonstrate effective communication skills and strategies.

Materials

This activity requires access to health resource materials.

Time

Each debate lasts 42 minutes.

Description of Activity

I find this activity useful in any content area that involves issues or dilemmas. I have used debate in family life, drug education, nutrition courses, and during units related to ethics, professional development, etc. Prior planning is essential to effectiveness. Students select topics from a list provided at the first of the term. For example, students in a family life course might select from a list that includes: Should condoms and other fertility control devices be distributed or available at public schools? Should HIV antibody testing be made mandatory in US colleges and universities? Should gay and lesbian couples be allowed to marry? Topics are assigned and students are grouped and notified of date of debate. Debate groups (usually about five students per group) are responsible for analyzing sources, synthesizing materials, dividing responsibilities, and presentation of concise and effective arguments. They must prepare both a pro and con argument. Students are not told which side they will argue until the date of the actual debate.

Procedure

1. Each group is informed of their respective positions at the start of class.

2. Preparation- Each group is given ten minutes to collect thoughts and finalize preparations. (Pro argument always presents position first)

3. Initial Remarks- One member of each group is given five minutes to introduce position.

4. Rebuttal- A second member of each group is given three minute to rebut opposition's initial remarks.

5. Questions- Third and fourth members of each group field questions from the audience for five minutes per position.

6. Closing argument- The final group member(s) is given three minutes to close.

Evaluation

I do not evaluate the debate based on debating skills. I evaluate this activity in the following manner. The debate is worth 150 points. Fifty points are dependent on the way in which the person presents his or her argument. Does he or she abide by instructions? Is argument relevant? Is the argument focused? Are communication skills and strategies effective? The paper counts for one hundred of the possible points. This paper provides a general consideration of the issue, construction of both supporting and opposing arguments, and, finally, a statement of the students' personal opinion regarding the issue. The paper and debate help the students develop the ability to view both sides of an issue before finalizing an opinion or position.

15

Action Packed Previews May Lead to Numerous Reviews

Submitted by Ladona Tornabene, Ph.D., CHES
University of South Dakota, Vermillion, SD

Part of communicating effectively is writing. Part of writing is knowing how to convey such passion for the subject matter that the reader is captivated by the introduction and compelled to read on and on and on... Sometimes getting started is the toughest part. The following activity is designed to spark creativity so as to help students begin writing on a topic of their choice related to health education.

Objectives

Students will watch and discuss a movie preview in order to stimulate creativity and generate interest when writing an introduction to a paper on a health-related topic of their choice.

Materials Needed

TV and VCR
paper and pencils
a movie preview
pens in various ink colors

Time Needed

Thirty minutes to one hour

Description of Activity

To fully illustrate the importance of a powerful introduction, show a movie preview (obtain permission first), then ask how many students would like to see that movie. Ask them why. Liken the movie preview to a good introduction of a paper. Discuss attention-grabbing ideas that would make the reader desire to read their papers, just as the movie preview made them desire to see the movie. Explain that the introduction is brief and use the analogy of the movie preview to provide further insight as to how the introduction has the ability to pull the reader into the "action," leaving them longing for more! The class will usually create an abundance of ideas sparked by the movie preview. Use these to challenge them in writing their introductions. Then have students actually write (print) an introduction to a paper regarding a selected topic in health education. Instructor should provide pencils and paper.

Population Variations   This can be used with nontraditional students by showing excerpts from movie classics or with students from different cultures by doing the same with foreign films. Other variations include showing more than one movie preview.

Evaluation

All students are to turn in their introductions upon completion to the instructor's desk (no names on papers). Instructor uses coding to identify students so that papers can be returned. After all students are finished (instructor may set time limit), distribute introductory papers with the understanding that no one is allowed to critique his/her own work. Have students read the introductions silently and give written feedback as to whether they would like to read the entire paper or not. If yes, have them write their reasons why. If no, give suggestions on how the author could improve this introduction to generate interest. If time permits, students may critique more than one paper using a different color ink from the first person who evaluated it. Collect all papers. Upon the dismissal of class, return papers to students who originally wrote them. Ask them to type and make necessary revisions according to the feedback they received from classmates and turn in at the following class along with their original papers and written comments.

Timelines and Murals
Submitted by John S. Carter, Ph.D.
The Citadel, Charleston, SC

Students often lack a historical perspective or an appreciation for how an academic field, discipline, or profession (such as public health, epidemiology, or any health-related science) developed over time.

Lesson Objectives

Upon completion of this lesson the student should be able to:

1. gain a deeper appreciation for people/events constructing a discipline's history;

2. integrate culture, art, and history into the study of health;

3. utilize computer and Internet resources;

4. appreciate cooperative learning and multiculturalism to a greater degree; and

5. perform library research and learn history of a particular area of health.

Materials Required

Each "team" will investigate a specific period of time, one area of health, or a particular disease or health problem from "beginning" to "end."

Time Allocations

This project is best assigned for an entire grading period extending over a number of weeks.

How to Present the Lesson

Students will create a timeline or mural of key events and people responsible. For example, construct a historical timeline of epidemiology or public health. Coverage of time periods, scientific discoveries, or significant contributors can randomly be accomplished through students and/or teams of "investigators."

Organization of Class

Individual, partners, or teams of 'historians' may be formed (dependent upon ages, grade levels, maturity, and interests of learners).

Variations for Different Populations

There are specific health problems and key individuals who model valuable qualities for all or some students (for example, African-Americans who contributed to solving health problems and epidemics may best be studied during African-American Awareness Month each February).

Evaluation Techniques

Students and teachers can evaluate finished projects during construction or when works are prominently displayed.

Alternative Healing

Submitted by Marilyn S. Massey, Ed.D., CHES
Texas Tech University, Lubbock, TX

As traditional medicine becomes even more expensive and, in some cases, ineffective, a growing number of people are seeking alternative healing methods to help with everyday health problems as well as with chronic diseases. For example, in 1990, Americans made approximately 425 million visits to alternative health practitioners, which was more than they made to primary care physicians. Additionally, in 1992, the Office of Alternative Medicine was established to explore unconventional healing methods such as meditation, massage, herbal therapy, acupuncture, and vitamin therapy (Gottlieb, 1995).

When teaching about health, alternative healing is an area that is often overlooked. This is unfortunate because individuals should be aware of choices they have with regard to their own preventative health care; thus, the world of alternative medicine is definitely worth exploring. This particular teaching strategy can be used within different topic areas such as cancer, cardiovascular disease, consumerism, noninfectious conditions, nutrition, and psychosocial health. It is designed to be flexible and to promote peer teaching and cooperative group learning.

Objectives

1. The student will be able to describe various forms of alternative healing.

2. The student will learn to appreciate the relevance of various natural forms of healing and the practitioners who offer these services.

3. The student will actively research and report key points regarding a specific form of alternative healing.

4. The student will effectively communicate researched information in both oral and written formats.

5. The student will work cooperatively within a small group.

Materials

1. Handouts on alternative healing-This introductory material can be photocopies of articles and/or book chapters as well as printed information from the Internet.

2. Slips of paper and a small box, students draw the slips of paper from the box to determine their assigned group topic.

3. Overhead transparency projector and screen (optional).

4. VCR & tape(s) that illustrate alternative healing methods (optional).

5. Paper & pens for taking notes

Time

The introduction of alternative healing and the explanation of the group project could cover one to two 50-minute class periods, depending how in-depth the introduction is. Then, students can be given additional class time (at the discretion of the instructor) to work with their groups on the assignment. This class time can include one or more trips to the library. Once reports begin, two reports can be presented in one 50-minute class period. As a summation, a group panel or roundtable discussion group can take place within one class period.

Description of Activity

Alternative healing is introduced and briefly discussed. This information can be presented through a combination of handout material, overhead transparencies, and brief videotape clips. Next, the class is divided into pairs or small groups of three. (The number of groups will vary according to class size.) Each group draws a slip of paper from a box to determine what particular alternative healing topic they will present to the rest of the class. Each group is responsible for researching and making a 20-minute presentation on their specific topic to the rest of the class. Examples of topics that can be included are: homeopathy, acupuncture, Ayurvedic medicine, herbal therapy, chiropractic treatment, aromatherapy, massage, hydrotherapy, vitamin therapy, naturopathy, therapeutic nutrition, midwifery, oriental medicine, meditation, Shamanic healing practices, Noetic sciences, imagery, etc. Advise the students to avoid a lecture presentation and to try to make the learning experience as active as possible for participants. Each group should be encouraged to create an interesting and motivating report, but they do not have to follow a set format. Evaluation sheets can be given to each group ahead of time so that participants will know how they're being evaluated. Also, group evaluation forms can be used so that each group member has an opportunity to confidentially evaluate other members of his/her assigned group. As mentioned under the **TIME** section, time can be allowed for planning and preparation (during class and/or outside of class). Then, each groups presents its lesson to the class. A typewritten paper with key information from the presentation will be presented to the instructor at the time of the presentation. Once all presentations have been given, a culminating activity can include inviting guest speakers to address various alternative healing topics. This class session can be conducted utilizing a group panel or a roundtable discussion format. It is important that students prepare questions for the speakers before the scheduled visit and that time is allowed for a brief Q & A session.

Evaluation

This component consists of three parts: 1) oral presentation (criteria can be determined by the students and the instructor); 2) typewritten paper that accompanies presentation; 3) 1-2 page response paper that students write to offer feedback regarding the effectiveness of the guest speakers.

Credits: *Gottlieb, B. (Ed.). (1995).* New Choices in Healing, *Emmaus, PA:Rodale Press.*

Wandering Through WONDER
Submitted by Rich Miller
George Mason University, Fairfax, VA

Students in a personal health course need to learn how to use health-related technology as one way to promote their health knowledge, attitudes and practices. A wonderful and educational way is to tap into databases held at the Centers for Disease Control (CDC). All that needs to be done is to connect to the WONDER site at the CDC, select a database, identify variables, and generate a report. Students will be exposed to up-to-date information in health promotion and disease prevention and also have the opportunity to discuss its significance to personal health.

Objectives

Students will be able to:

1. demonstrate a proficiency in health education-related technology by accessing CDC's WONDER site on the internet,

2. analyze current CDC data in health promotion and disease prevention, and

3. discuss the how the data results are significant to their personal health.

Materials

Students will need to utilize a microcomputer or computer terminal with appropriate telecommunication and World Wide Web browser software to connect to the internet and reach the location, http://www.wonder.cdc.gov.

Instructions

As a virtual assignment in the study of health/safety conditions such as sexual transmitted diseases, students are instructed to connect to the internet using a World Wide Web browser, such as Netscape Navigator, and connect to the location, http://wonder.cdc.gov. Once they reach the site, they log in as an anonymous user. The directions for logging-in, selecting a database and generating a report are clearly presented on WONDER's homepage. Students are encouraged to practice connecting to WONDER and its many databases as wellas links to other CDC-related sites such as Morbidity and Mortality Weekly Report. Once students have developed confidence in using WONDER, they are ready to take-on a fun and informative assignment. Here are the steps:

1. Students need to develop at question that can be answered by examining CDC data bases. For example, they may wish to answer: How many US cases of AIDS have been reported to the CDC?

2. Students need to select the appropriate database to answer the question. In this example, they would select the Public USE AIDS database.

3. Students indicate how the incidence data should be arranged by demographic variables (gender, age, race, etc.). For instance, AIDS cases from 1990 to 1994 could be arranged according to age.

4. Students generate the report so that it appears in table format. This is done simply by clicking a screen button (Send Report) displayed by WONDER. Within seconds the table of AIDS cases appears on screen.

5. Students should instruct WONDER to email the results to them. They have an option of three table formats: ASCII (text), HTML (hypertext for web browsing) or RTF (rich text for conversion into word processing programs). For the simple purposes of this assignment, students should opt for ASCII. Students need to type in their email address and click the email screen button. Within seconds the table will arrive at their email account.

6. After receiving the email from the CDC, the students should forward it to their instructor.

Forwarding email is a standard function in all email programs. While doing so, the sender has the opportunity to attach a note to or insert (type) in a remark within the email file.

The students need to address the following questions in their attachment remark:

1. What was the question posed to WONDER (e.g., How many U.S. cases of AIDS have been reported to the CDC?)?

2. Why did the students pose this particular question to WONDER?

3. What is the answer to the question as displayed in the table?

4. What does this answer mean to the students' personal health?

Evaluation

Evaluation of this assignment is based on students' completion of this excursion through WONDER as well as their forwarding of adequate an appropriate responses to the four questions listed above. The instructor should peruse the forwarded table and attachment/remark and reply back (or forward back) to the students with constructive comments about this "technological achievement" and acknowledge its significance to personal health.

Examining the Origin and Impact of Life-style Habits

Submitted by Peggy J. Pedersen, Ph.D., CHES
Northern Illinois University, DeKalb, IL

Understanding the origin of some of their common life-style habits can assist students in understanding how habits develop over time and the impact of environmental and social learning influences. Students often are not patient with the process of change or appreciative of the origin of many of their habits, whether they be health enhancing or health compromising. This activity is designed to enable students to explore the origin of some of their health behaviors as well as to recognize how long they have been working on developing some of their current health habits. This activity can also serve as a vehicle for discussing why some students haven't adopted the habits of their family of origin and what factors played into their decision to act differently.

Objectives

At the completion of this activity students will be able to:

1. identify the health habits of their family of origin,

2. compare and contrast their current health habits with those of their family of origin,

3. discuss the impact their family's life-style habits have on the development of their own health habits, and

4. summarize the impact (both positive and negative) their current life-style habits may have on their health in the long term.

Materials/Time

Students will need a copy of the Life-style Habits Worksheet. This worksheet generally takes 5-10 minutes to complete. Twenty to thirty minutes should be provided for students to develop their written evaluation or the evaluation can be completed orally in small groups, followed by a class summary and discussion. Total activity time = 45-60 minutes.

Activity Presentation

Review with students that absence of disease does not equate to wellness. Diseases related to life-style develop gradually over time and we can often be lulled into a false sense of security during young adulthood and middle age.

Ask students to examine the current life-style habits of their immediate family (parents, siblings) using the Life-style Habits Worksheet. For each family member, place a check in the appropriate box if that family member practices the described action.

Note: If students have children and a family of their own, you may want to suggest they analyze their present family life-style habits and the impact they will potentially have on their children if they choose to adopt them.

Evaluation

Ask students to respond to the questions below either orally or in writing.

Compare and contrast your current life-style habits with those of your family of origin. Summarize the contribution and the impact (both positive and negative) of your family's life-style habits on your current habits. What implications are there for your health in the long term?

Life-style Habit Worksheet

Have the students prepare a worksheet table, listing the life-style habits in the left column and heading the remaining columns with the family member category (father, mother, sister, brother, self, other, other, other).

Life-style Habits: Eats 2-4 servings of fruit, eats 3-5 servings of vegetables, limits dietary fat intake, smokes, chews tobacco, is addicted to other substance, exercises regularly, gets annual checkups, does monthly BSE (females) or TSE (males), gets blood pressure checked, has blood lipid / cholesterol screen, battles verbally when angry, battles physically when angry, avoids people when angry, cries openly when sad or upset, discusses feelings when sad or upset, avoids people when sad or upset, talks openly about any topic, wears seat belt, wears helmet if biking or on motorcycle, and follows posted speed limit.

Smoking Risk Factors

Submitted by Kristine Brown, Ph.D., CHES
Florida Atlantic University, Davie, FL

Feelings of infallibility are a major reason for college students engaging in unhealthy behaviors. Emphysema is one of several health risks associated with smoking that does not develop until after years of smoking. This activity is designed to give students somewhat of an idea of what it's like to live with emphysema.

Objective

Following completion of this activity, students will be able to:

1. Identify various risk factors associated with smoking.

Materials Needed

Small coffee straws enough for each student (straws can be cut into sections).

Estimated Time

5 to 10 minutes

Description of Activity

1. Brainstorm a list of health problems that have been shown to be associated with smoking.

2. Discuss emphysema (what happens to the lungs, the symptoms, etc.).

3. Pass out straws to each student; Have students hold their nose and breath through the straw for 60 seconds.

4. Ask students to do 5 jumping jacks while breathing through the straw.

5. Ask students for their reaction. How did they feel? (several students will not be able to breath through the straw and will feel like they're suffocating).

6. Ask students to imagine how difficult and uncomfortable it would be to breath like that day after day. Ask how this would limit their abilities to engage in even simple activities such as walking up a few stairs.

7. Explain that people in the last stages of emphysema experience not only difficulty breathing, but pain with each breath as well.

Evaluation

Have students write a brief reaction to the activity.

21

Learn to Teach Tobacco Cessation Classes
Submitted by John S. Carter, Ph.D.
The Citadel, Charleston, SC

In certain segments of the population, all forms of tobacco usage are on the rise. Generally, peer teachers have been an effective methodology in convincing other young people to stop using (or not use) tobacco products.

Lesson Objectives

Upon completion of this lesson the student should be able to:

1. become a peer teacher and facilitator of tobacco cessation courses in their school and community,

2. enhance written and oral communication skills, and

3. experience satisfaction and sense of accomplishment by helping someone overcome a health problem.

Materials Required

Health educators need simply to contact local offices of The American Cancer Society (ACS) or The American Lung Association (ALA). These organizations can design facilitator training classes for young people, or instruct the health teacher how to "educate" volunteer peer/student facilitators to lead smoking cessation classes for the school and/or community.

Time Allocations

The planning process needs to occur at least one-half year in advance of actual facilitation; this allows adequate training time, as well as opportunities for "trainees" to practice and observe real classes led by a trained facilitator.

How to Present the Lesson

Not everyone will want (or should) be a peer facilitator. Ideally, ex-users make good teachers of substance cessation. Rather than a required component of a health course, use this "activity" as an extra assignment or perhaps as one of a group of optional choices of semester-long projects.

Variations for different populations

Tobacco cessation courses can be team-taught by student/peer facilitators. At-risk populations should be aggressively targeted for these classes.

Evaluation Techniques

The ACS and ALA provide client evaluation forms. Local forms can also be developed to assess not only facilitator effectiveness, but client success. Short- and long-term follow-up with ex-tobacco users is imperative. The weeks and months immediately after quitting tobacco are periods of greatest recidivism; formation and subsequent facilitation of support groups are vital, and offer still another way to involve students.

22

Visit a Soup Kitchen or a Shelter

Submitted by John S. Carter, Ph.D.
The Citadel, Charleston, SC

Young people often adopt an attitude **of** invincibility, believing that 'it can never happen to me'. Young people also experiment with alcohol, tobacco, and drugs, usually under the misimpression that they will get this phase out of their system while they're young. Most individuals believe that they'll simply be able to walk away from substance use/ misuse/abuse once they "get older."

Lesson Objectives

Upon completion of this lesson the student should be able to:

1. learn about how alcohol/tobacco/drug use, and/or poor health habits/behaviors affect real human lives;

2. reinforce the major goal of a personal health class ... to help people make sound decisions (and not repeat painful mistakes of others);

3. appreciate "that were it not for the Grace of God, there would go I" (spiritual health); and

4. demonstrate a sense of community service.

Materials Required

Each student can contribute in some way to the purchase of food, or preparation/service of a meal at a soup kitchen/shelter.

Time Allocations

Two to three hours should be spent at a morning, noon, or evening mealtime.

How to Present the Lesson

Organization of Class: Arrangement for one's class to serve in a voluntary role should be coordinated with the director of volunteer programs at the shelter or soup kitchen. Determine dates and times when your group (or individuals) is needed, how many patrons to prepare for, menu preferences, etc. In lieu of a group effort, individual volunteer assistance will serve the same purpose.

It might be wise for the teacher to have a "trial run" prior to the group's visit just to check details, i.e.., where to park, what entrance to use, if adequate paper products and serving equipment are available, and what pre-preparation/cooking can be done beforehand.

Evaluation Techniques

Each student should write a 1-2 page report about his/her experience and impressions. When possible, each paper should feature one guest's "story." Classroom discussions of experiences are perhaps more valuable than the necessary grading of papers for content and mechanics.

Need and Conceptualization of the Personal Drug Philosophy Activity

Submitted by Ray Tricker, Ph.D., CHES
Oregon State University, Corvallis, OR

At the college level, it is important that students continue to examine the issues of drug use and abuse from a variety of different perspectives. The purpose of this activity is to provide opportunities for students to examine issues related to drugs from a personal perspective. The drug philosophy activity **is** a statement of the students personal relationship or experiences related to alcohol, medications, street drugs, and where applicable to others in the students' life who use drugs. Furthermore, through this activity students are encouraged to develop critical thinking about their values related to drugs and examine how these values influence their behavior and the behavior of others.

Objectives

Through the completion of this activity students will:
1. clarify their values related to their own use of drugs;
2. clarify their values related to the drug use of others;
3. describe the characteristics of influential significant others in their lives who influenced drug use or cessation of drug use;
4. describe how they would deal with a close friend or family member who uses drugs;
5. describe the guidelines, or personal rules that they have established to guide them toward responsible, healthy involvement with drugs; and
6. review their former attitudes, values, behaviors and future intentions with regard to drug use.

Procedures

The activity can be introduced in class through discussion of the five most important factors in the students' life. Students suggest each factor, such as a spiritual belief, money, friends, family, a career, marriage, children, travel etc. (Three columns are drawn on the chalk board.) These important personal factors are written on the chalk board in the first column. The class is asked next to suggest the top five values of a drug abuser/addict. When at least ten different factors have been recorded in each of the two columns students are asked to comment on the similarities/disparities existing between the values of the two groups. The purpose of this aspect is to illustrate the significance of drugs in the lives of the abuser/addict.

Following this activity students are asked to submit a written, personal philosophy clarifying those factors that have significantly influenced their involvement or noninvolvement with drugs. In their philosophy paper students are asked to address the following issues.

1. Why the student has chosen to use or not use drugs.

2. What guidelines or personal rules does the student have for their own purposes related to drug use.

3. Comment on the possibility for future change in the currently held philosophy.

4. Describe any people the student has known who influenced the use or non-use of drugs.

5. How do you, would YOU relate to someone you knew well who was abusing drugs?

6. How would you confront a close friend or family member who you knew was abusing drugs?

Evaluation Criteria

Student should clearly understand that their grade for this assignment is not based upon lengths or whether their opinions, values or beliefs agree with those of the professor. The evaluation is based upon evidence that the student has clearly thought through his/her perceptions related to the philosophy statement. Also, content and depth of the analysis, clear articulation, reference to personal examples and discussion of the students' perceptions are used to evaluate the quality of this assignment. Students are told that papers should be **full** of content, well articulated, illustrated and substantiated with personal examples. These criteria are clearly presented in the form of a compulsory assignment, with the outline for the course at the beginning of the term. Students are informed that their papers are strictly confidential and that after reading and evaluation will be destroyed unless they wish to collect the paper after it has been graded. This provides each student with the security that the information they disclose will not be published or conveyed to any other individual.

24

Around the World of Addictions: An Adolescent Perspective

Submitted by Dr. Helen M. Welle
Georgia Southern University, Statesboro, GA
and
Kathleen O'Rourke, MS
State University of New York at Potsdam

Highschool students operate from a variety of constructs concerning substance abuse and addiction. In recent years, prevalence rates of illicit drug use among high school students has declined considerably, yet addictive behaviors and addictions among this same population have increased substantially. The youth of today need to rethink their assumptions about addictions, in order to redefine who is at risk and effectively address the underlying causes of addictions.

Objective

Students will redefine their assumptions concerning addictions and addicts. Students will be able to: 1) list descriptor terms for a variety of substance and behavioral addictions, 2) determine common characteristics among all the addictions, 3) describe the addictive process, and 4) construct a profile of the high school student whose at high risk for addictive behavior.

Grade Level   High School Students (but adaptable to any age group).

Material and Timeframe

Poster boards (or large sheets of paper) and markers. Handouts explaining addictions. A charismatic leader with high tolerance for movement and noise.

Teaching Activity

The focal concept of this interactive activity is to challenge high school students to reconstruct their assumptions concerning addictions and addictive behaviors. High school students, operating from a dichotomous learning modality, characterize addictions/addicts as bad and consequently assess their personal risk for addiction as low. Yet, when one looks at characteristics of addicts, ie. low self-esteem, feelings of powerlessness, unresolved issues, high degree of turmoil, etc; teenagers emerge as a particularly vulnerable group . The Health Belief Model instructs health teachers that unless students believe their susceptibility to be high, risk avoidance/reduction educational strategies will not be effective or heeded. This activity encourages students to rethink or "reconstruct" their ideas of addictions and addicts to realize that all teenagers are at risk. Health educators can use this realization as the foundation to formulate antidrug/ anti-addictive education strategies relevant to this age category.

The activity is introduced to the students with a brief discussion of addictions, both substance and behaviorally based. The students are divided into five or six groups of equal size. Each group is given a piece of paper (poster board size) and a marker, assigned a different addiction, i.e. caffeine, tobacco, alcohol, exercise, food, etc., and writes the addiction across the top of the paper. Each group chooses a "runner", a person who will bring the sheet of paper clockwise to the group next to them when the instructor yells "switch."

The activity is initiated when the teacher says "go." Each group has a few seconds to write the characteristics of an individual addicted to the behavior listed at the top of the paper. At the "switch" command, the runner gives the paper to the group adjacent to them, rotating a new paper and addiction to each group. Group members then add characteristics to the list before them, trying to avoid looking at any of the previously written descriptors already on the paper. This exchange continues until all groups have seen each addiction and responded to it. The "runner" then returns to their original group.

The instructor then collects all sheets of paper, chooses and reads several of the descriptors listed on each sheet aloud (yet keeps the topic of addiction hidden). Students are asked to guess which addiction the instructor is currently describing (students who wrote the descriptors for that particular addiction are not allowed to guess, although this is somewhat tough to enforce).

Evaluation Technique/Closure

Evaluation methods of this teaching activity tend to be more qualitative and process oriented. The authors' personal experiences with use of this teaching technique reveal that the students call out a variety of addiction for each list of descriptors. Discussion ensues regarding addictive behavior and students generally come to the realization that it is behavior that is "abusive," not any particular drug. A consolidation of the descriptors, a natural closing to this activity, usually is instrumental in building a 'profile' of high risk individuals. High school students realize that this profile could be describing a number of individuals, possibly themselves.

Side Note   An alternative way to conduct this activity is to ask the students, rather than give descriptors of addicts, to list negative or positive affects involvement in the addictive behavior. Once again, positive behaviors are similar for all addictions (i.e. whether using alcohol or exercise, self-confidence is bolstered). This is followed by a discussion of how to use positive health behaviors in a nonaddictive manner to reach these goals.

25

The Mirror Technique
Submitted by Kristine Brown, Ph.D., CHES
Florida Atlantic University, Boca Raton, FL

Active listening is a critical component of effective conflict resolution skills. Many people become angry when they feel that their partner is not listening more so than from the actual incident (e.g. roommate not asking permission before borrowing something). People often forget what the argument was about but they don't forget the feelings of frustration and anger that result. Feeling validated helps alleviate feelings of frustration and anger, thereby increasing the potential for effective communication and conflict resolution.

Objectives
Following completion of the activity, students will be able to:
1. demonstrate the Mirror Technique of communicating, and
2. understand and demonstrate the difference between hearing and listening.

Materials Needed
None

Estimated Time
15 minutes

Description of Activity
1. Ask what the difference is between hearing and listening. Brainstorm a list of qualities of a good listener.
2. Explain that when we look in a mirror, we merely see a reflection of ourselves.
3. Explain that the "Mirror Technique" is when we paraphrase or simply reflect the feelings of our partner without including any of our own feelings.

4. Have students pair up; Each pair consists of a Sender and a Receiver; On your cue, the Sender in each pair will talk about anything (preferably a situation in which they were angry) for 60 seconds (or shorter); The Receiver is to keep in mind the attributes of a good listener.

5. After 60 seconds, the Receiver will paraphrase what was said. They may include interpretations such as "you seem to be angry when your friend said ..." They will conclude by stating, "Is that right?"

6. Ask how the Sender felt when they were given the opportunity to talk and when the Receiver was paraphrasing back to them.

7. Ask how the Receiver felt when they were listening and when they were paraphrasing back.

Evaluation

1. Assign the students the task of practicing the Mirror Technique during the following week and report back to the class.

26

Define Sexual Harassment
Submitted by John S. Carter, Ph.D.
The Citadel, Charleston, SC

Clearly defineable answers to questions about what is acceptable and unacceptable behavior are important to all individuals (particularly so for males). It cost American companies $24.3 million to settle sexual harassment cases in 1995.

Lesson Objectives

Upon completion of this lesson the student should be able to:
1. address a difficult area with less fear,
2. open up and talk about a controversial topic,
3. enjoy less threat and intimidation than many people feel about the subject of sexual harassment,
4. enhance written and oral communication skills, and
5. appreciate more multidisciplined activities and learning.

Materials Required

"The Sexual Harassment Prevention Game," by Chuck Hatten, Seattle, Washington; $600 for 5 packets of case studies.

Time Allocations

Semester- or unit-long assignments can be presented at the conclusion of the grading period.

How to Present the Lesson

In lieu of $600, students are assigned to create, write, and present case studies, scenarios, and perform role playing. Writing and directing plays which depict common situations are also encouraged. Because a multidisciplinary approach is an objective, students should seek advice through legal precedents, interviews, and study of business administration cases.

Organization of Class

Individual, partners, or teams may be formed (dependent upon ages, grade levels, maturity, and interests of learners).

Evaluation Techniques

In addition to grading student "research" presentations, a pre- and post-experience exam can be administered to measure student change in knowledge, attitudes, and behaviors concerning the topic of sexual harassment.

Credits.   *This idea came from an article written by Daryl Strickland of the* Seattle Times *which appeared in the* Post & Courier Newspaper *in Charleston, SC on 17 March 1996.*

27

Prejudice

Submitted by Cathie Stivers, Ph.D., CHES
Longwood College, Farmville, VA

We often learn new information by associating it with something we already know, this allows us to learn the new information quicker and retain it longer. When we use this same learning method with new people, however, the risk of prejudice or "prejudging" increases, even when no harm is intended. Indeed, first impressions hold fast and are difficult to dispel, especially if they provide the only information upon which long-term opinions are formed.

While the history of the United States is replete with prejudice, the global relationships we now experience through computers, media, trade, and politics have brought us face to face with many people who are different from us. What appears to be a consequent increase in prejudice and hatred in the last decade may be an increase in visibility rather than in frequency or degree. Tension, fear, and misinformation become key ingredients in the recipe for prejudice, and possibly hate.

In order to prevent prejudice, one must talk about it. In order to talk about it, discussion must be introduced in such a way that people do not feel they must defend themselves or that they are being judged, moralized, or blamed. In other words, people must believe that their behavior isn't "bad," just human. This activity provides a neutral, non-hostile, yet revealing mechanism, by which participants discover that they are victims as well as a perpetrators of prejudice, no matter how "good" they are.

Objectives

At the conclusion of this activity the student will:

1. understand that prejudice is simply "pre-judging," born out of error, and rarely born out of true hate;

2. understand that prejudices become harmful if they prevent him/her from learning more about other people and their differences;

3. be able to give at least one example each of when someone "pre-judged" him/her, and when he/she "pre-judged" someone else;

4. be able to describe practical ways in which the formation of new relationships with people different from him/her isn't inhibited by prejudice; and

5. be able to give examples of diversity or difference other than race/ethnicity, age, gender, religion, sexual orientation, and socioeconomic status.

Materials Needed

1 sheet of paper, blank on both sides, per student

1 blank index card per student

1 #2 pencil per student

Time Needed

50 minutes - 1 hr. and 15 minutes

Activity

"What you see may not be me."

Step 1: Instructor to students: "On the provided paper, anonymously and briefly answer these questions: (a) Do you consider yourself to be a prejudiced person? Why or why not? (b) What is your opinion of prejudiced people? Have students put this aside for later.

Step 2: Instructor has students count off "1, 2, 1, 2" etc. to form two groups. (For a little more fun, use something like "Batman, Robin" or "Salt, Pepper" or "Clinton, Dole" instead.)

Step 3: Instructor to students: "On the provided index card, write which group you're in. Then *legibly:*

Batman group: Write down something about yourself that you don't think we'd guess about you, that you're willing to share. (Examples: "I'm a certified EMT." "I like classical music." "I work part-time at a flower shop.")

Robin group: Write down a brief description of an instance in which you were mistaken for someone or something that you are *not,* and tell how you felt about it." (Examples: "I used to have long hair. At a mall, a girl asked me for an autograph, thinking I was a rock star. I was embarrassed but amused." "I'm often mistaken for my sister. I don't like it because I don't look a thing like her, and I'm tired of being recognized as 'her sister' instead of *me.*" *"I* was mistaken for being mean. It bothered me. I'm not mean, I'm just quiet.")

Step 4: Instructor collects Batman index cards, tells Robins to keep their cards. Instructor shuffles the Batman cards, and distributes one to each Robin (if there is an odd number of students, the instructor can participate).

Step 5: Instructor to Robins: each of you holds the card of a Batman in this room. Find the Batman whose card you hold. When you find him or her, give your card to that Batman, so that each of you has the other one's card." Instructor allows for the few minutes it will take for these pairs to form.

Step 6: Instructor to Robins: tell your Batman about what you've written on your card." Instructor allows a few minutes for this exchange.

Step 7: Instructor poses questions: (a)   "Robins, how many attempts did you make before you found the right Batman? What where you looking for in trying to find this Batman? Why did you ask the person or the people that you asked?" (b) "Bat-people, were you asked more than once about a description that was not yours? How did you feel about it? What did your Robin's card say?"

Step 8: Instructor debriefs students on the purpose of the activity in which they just participated: 'You've now seen how easy it is to 'pre-judge' someone. Probably every one of us in this room has at least one time in our lives been mistaken for someone or something we weren't. Likewise, we have each undoubtedly been in a situation where we had to guess about a person we didn't know because we had nothing to base our knowledge of them on except our hunches. In either case, 'prejudging' occurs. The word 'prejudice' means 'pre-judge,' and so now you can see that we've all been victims of, as well as perpetrators of, prejudice at some point in our lives. Our pre-judging doesn't mean we are bad or hateful, necessarily. It is only when prejudices prevent us from learning more about other people and their differences that they become harmful."

Step 9: Instructor continues: 'Before we talk more about prejudice, take the paper on which you answered the first two questions, turn it over, and answer these questions:

1. After this activity, do you consider yourself to be a prejudiced person? Why or why not?"

2. "Did your answer change from before the activity?"

3. "Has your opinion of prejudiced people changed since before the activity?"

Step 10: Instructor discusses practices which prevent prejudice from interfering with the formation of relationships with people who are different from us (*About Understanding Diversity,* 1993).

1. Ask and invite questions about your differences, and be open and honest about them.

2. Don't assume anything about the person's wishes, preferences, or beliefs. If you don't know, ask. Chances are the person will be more offended if you don't ask and just assume, than if you do ask.

3. Avoid implying or perceiving anyone to be a spokesperson for his or her group based solely on one characteristic. To ask "How do African-Americans feel about that?" is as senseless as asking "How do men feel about that?"

4. Don't make jokes at the expense of someone else, their group, or even your own group. Even in jest, these jokes can be very hurtful. Furthermore, if you hear someone else telling a racist, sexist, or other -ist joke, call them on it. Your silence allows it to continue, whether your approve of the joke or not.

5. Broaden your horizons. Learn more about other groups via public radio and television broadcasts, museum exhibits and performances of art, music and theater from different cultures, alternative press publications, workshops and other forms of continuing education, travel, volunteer work, attendance at organizational meetings, etc.

6. Don't just tolerate diversity, celebrate it! Be proud of yourself and of others, and enjoy each other's differences as much as your similarities.

Evaluation

1. Steps 1 and 9 can serve as a pre- and post-measure of objectives 3 and 5.

2. Written test questions can measure objectives 1 through 5.

Credits: *About Understanding Diversity, (1993). Booklet # 490498-10-92. South Deerfield, MA: Channing L. Bete Co., Inc.*

Subjective Decision Making and HIV Risk Among College Students

Submitted by Donna A. Champeau, Ph.D., CHES
Oregon State University, Corvallis, OR

It is well known that college students engage in high levels of unsafe sexual behavior that put them at risk for HIV infection. In order to reduce the amount of unsafe sex exhibited by many college students, it is necessary to help the student understand how the subjective nature of their decisions may put them at risk. This activity is designed to enable the student to examine their own subjective belief system as it pertains to what they perceive to be aspects of a "safe" partner. It is also a lesson that will depict how fast HIV can spread in any population.

Objectives

At the completion of this activity students will be able to:

1. identify the subjective-based criteria a person might use to determine if a potential sex partner is infected with HIV,

2. identify the objective criteria used to determine the safety factor of a potential sex partner, and

3. explain the potential danger of incorrect subjective judgment in terms of the spread of HIV in a population.

Materials

Bromothymol Blue

Sodium bicarbonate water

clear plastic glasses

distilled water

eye dropper

overhead projector

Preparation

Poor distilled water into 12 plastic cups, each about 1/3 full. In 2 of the cups, put the sodium bicarbonate water, 1/3 full. Place the cups on a table in front of the class or somewhere easily accessible.

Activity Presentation

Discuss with students the things about a person that would make them believe that a potential partner is "safe" or free from HIV infection. Point out the criteria that is objective and subjective in nature. (example: The way one dresses, or where they live would be subjective whereas an HIV test result would be objective.) After this discussion, explain to the class that you are going to demonstrate how incorrect subjective evaluation can be potentially harmful when choosing a sex partner and engaging in unprotected sex, however, college students tend to engage in unprotected sex at a very high rate (cite research here).

1. Have 14 volunteers come up and take a cup from the table (keep track of who takes the 2 sodium bicarbonate glasses).

2. Split the class in two groups and explain that they are at a party, or function where one might be tempted to find a potential sex partner. Tell them that they are going to choose three different people from the other group to exchange body fluids with.

3. Have them mix liquid in their cup with three other people from the other group, then have them stand back by their group.

4. Now comes the fun part! Have each person come up and place their glass on the overhead projector. Take the eyedropper and put a drop of bromothymol blue into the cup. If the clear liquid turns blue, they are infected, if it turns pink, they are not.

5. Once everyone is tested, count how many infections occurred with just 2 infected individuals. What are the implications here? You may want the students to try and figure out who the infected individuals are, but this is a side issue that is not important for these objectives.

Evaluation

- Have the students discuss why they hypothetically chose the individuals they did.

- Have the students list the subjective and objective criteria for making good decisions about safe sex practices with regards to HIV infection.

- Discuss the factors that contribute to an individual's engaging in unsafe sex practices, and the risk involved.

References: Williams, S. S., et al., (1992). College *Students Use Implicit Personality Theory Instead of Safer Sex.* **Journal of Applied Social Psychology.** 22. 12 921-933.

Note: This lesson was adapted from an integrated science lesson. Unknown source.

29

Reducing Homophobia in the Classroom

Submitted by Linda A. Berne, Ed.D., CHES
The University of North Carolina at Charlotte, NC

Many students bring strong negative attitudes about homosexuality and homosexuals to the college campus. To facilitate harmony and justice among students, campus health educators need strategies for programs to deal effectively with prejudicial attitudes and to handle potential conflict during such programming. The two activities presented help leaders work with heterosexuals to explore their attitudes toward homosexuality and develop empathy with gay and lesbian peers. An intervention sequence is recommended to cope with hostility from antagonistic participants and to work through the controversy to reach desired outcomes. Key Words:
> *homosexuality,*
> *homophobia,*
> *college students, and*
> *sexual orientation*

Most students come to colleges and universities from families with Judeo-Christian values where homosexuality is condemned. As a result, students often mirror strong negative attitudes toward gays, lesbians and bisexuals (GLB), without giving the matter any significant or personal thought. While some secondary schools have implemented programs supportive of GLB youth most have limited the issue to the context of risky behaviors, or avoided it completely. Therefore, our university classes or campus programs may be the first time students have truly had an opportunity to understand and appreciate diversity in sexual orientation.

Many students are not aware of the devastating health consequences suffered by GLB living in a homophobic society. GLB are three to seven times more likely to attempt/commit suicide; more likely to abuse alcohol and drugs; more likely to suffer from identity confusion, low self esteem and attendant mental health complications; more likely to be runaways, throwaways and prostitutes; and less likely to get appropriate medical care.

Researchers generally place the number of gays and lesbians between 4% to 10% of the population, but many high school and college students would swear they have never met anyone who is gay. The reasons are at least twofold. Gay youths spend much of their adolescence trying to figure out their own sexual orientation. Many withdraw in confusion, appearing to be shy, not gay. Others initially attempt heterosexual relationships and are thought to be heterosexual by their peers. By the time GLB confirm their orientations, they may be nearly out of high school or college. Secondly, because the negative stigma attached to homosexuality is so great in most school cultures (particularly among male athletes, religious right groups and Greeks), gays and lesbians spend much of their time pretending to be heterosexual to avoid ridicule, condemnation and even bodily harm.

It is not unusual for the college environment to be the first place gays and lesbians attempt to come out of the closet in search of like-oriented friends and lovers. The trauma in this process depends on the support they perceive from roommates, peers, teachers, mentors and their own families. Educators can help both gay/lesbian and heterosexual youths develop healthier attitudes toward their own orientation and tolerance and concern for others. It can be done by exploring attitudes toward homosexuality and heterosexuality, through case studies, empathy experiences and ultimately through contacts with GLB peers. Hopefully heterosexual students from traditional backgrounds will open the door of tolerance wide enough to accept their gay friends, family members, and peers who already have been a part of their lives, but who have not been able to share their total identities. Only through disclosure and subsequent communication can understanding at the personal level really begin.

The two activities below are designed to help heterosexual young people understand their attitudes toward homosexuality and to develop empathy for others who perceive their sexuality through a different lens. "Walk a Mile in My Shoes," should be introduced before students know the lesson deals with homosexuality so they will give their natural responses to the case studies posed. "Do You Contribute to Homophobia?" heightens student awareness to a variety of attitudes toward homosexuality including biases in both directions on the continuum.

Many health educators are reluctant to deal with homosexuality other than dispensing facts because they feel unsure of their ability to deal with conflict and hot emotions in the classroom. Altercations between outspoken religious right students and gay activists, while not necessarily negative if well handled, are an ever increasing probability. The final part of this paper gives leaders a strategy to employ when emotions run hot. If practiced effectively, it can calm the situation, help students think before they run off at the mouth, and assure that all students will be heard and respected.

While it is not the health educator's role to tell students what they should and should not believe, leaders have a moral obligation to help students gain knowledge, examine their own values and to protect the dignity and self worth of all students. These two strategies plus "Homosexuality: Exploring Your Feelings," provide three lessons to that end.

Activity 1

Walk A Mile In My Shoes

Objectives

The students will: (1) observe the heterosexcentric bias inherent in our culture, and (2) question the justice of discrimination based on sexual orientation.

Materials

Tape player, audio tape "Walk a Mile in My Shoes" by Joe South, lyrics of music, one copy of each scenario on large note cards.

Time

30-45 minutes, depending on time spent processing.

Procedures

While students enter the room, play the music, "Walk a Mile in My Shoes." Tell the group that they are going to help some people make decisions based on the information provided. Students are to put themselves in the roles of the characters and make a decision regarding the questions asked. Place students in groups of 4-6, giving each group one of the scenarios provided below. After about 8-10 minutes, ask each group to read their situation to the class and render their decision.

Next, explain that each of the situations involve gays and lesbians, and that these situations were real life events. Go over each with the processing cue and ask: Does this information change your mind about your decision? Why, or why not? Give students time to confer for responses. Summarize with the following questions: (1) Do you think gays and lesbians have the same thoughts, feelings and desires as heterosexuals? (2) Do you think that gays and lesbians have the same range of goals, hopes and dreams as the range for heterosexuals? (3) Has society benefited by having different "rules" for gays and lesbians? (4) How would society be different if gays and lesbians had the same rights as heterosexuals? How would the lives of gays and lesbians be different? (5) What would it be like to spend 24 hours in the shoes of a closeted gay or lesbian person? An openly gay or lesbian person?

Jack and Shelly have been dating for two years and have been seeing each other exclusively for the last year and a half. Jack has been out of college for 5 years and has built a small, but successful architectural firm in the city. Shelly has been teaching 2 years at a nearby elementary school. Both have been saving for their future dream home and have a nest egg of about $20,000. They love each other and see a bright future together. In your judgment, are Jack and Shelly ready for marriage? How would you rate them as candidates for marriage, from the information given?

Processing cue: Jack and Shelly are both males. Most states do not recognize same sex marriages.

Three couples go out together to an upscale restaurant for dinner and drinks. They request three checks when ordering. After the meal the waiter/waitress brings the checks. To whom should he/she give them?

Processing cue: One couple is heterosexual, one couple is gay and one couple is lesbian.

Theo and Nicole have two children, Andy age 4, and Kali age 2. Nicole has a part-time job so that she can spend more time with the kids. Theo has a relatively high pressure job, but makes reasonable money. Theo comes home and tells Nicole that there is an opportunity for a transfer and promotion, with a $12K salary increase and all moving expenses paid. The new job is in a city similar to the one where they live now. In your opinion, should Nicole agree to the move?

Processing cue: Theodora and Nicole are a lesbian couple with two children, both Theo's.

Theo and Nicole have two children, Andy age 4 and Kali age 2. Nicole has a part-time job so that she can spend more time with the kids. Theo has a relatively high pressure job, but makes reasonable money. Since Nicole has moved to part time work, she has poor benefits. Theo wants to change the health care coverage to a family plan, covering Nicole and the kids. A good idea?

Processing cue: Theodora and Nicole are a lesbian couple. Most companies do not cover nonmarital partners. Theo can only cover herself and the children.

> Austin grew up in the Lutheran Church and always felt that church offered a special and unique relationship for people. After high school, he went to college and majored in Civil Engineering. While in the Persian Gulf War, Austin had a life changing spiritual experience. During the next six months, Austin's friends and fellow officers urged him to seriously consider a career shift to the ministry. It is three years later, and Austin still feels led to help others expand their relationship with God and with each other. He is highly effective in reaching out to people spiritually and personally. He has talked it over with his wife, and she is supportive. Would you recommend Austin for seminary training and a parish?

Processing cue: Austin is a closeted bisexual male who practices heterosexual monogamy with his wife.

After processing each case study above, introduce students to the following terms and their definitions.

1. Homophobia - irrational fears of homosexuality in others, fear of homosexual feelings within oneself, or selfloathing because of one's homosexuality. There is no acceptance of the person or the behavior .

2. Homosexual bias - belief that homosexual behavior is wrong based on religious or other tenets; however there is acceptance of the person, but rejection of the behavior.

3. Heterosexism - the belief that heterosexuality is the only valid and acceptable orientation, superior to homosexuality.

4. Heterosexcentrism- assuming that everyone is heterosexual, and basing all aspects of culture and life-style on this assumption.

Summarize the major points to questions 1-5 above. Close by asking the students to listen to the music again.

Activity 2

Do You Contribute to Homophobia?

Objectives

The students will (1) accurately sort card statements along a continuum from homophobia to hemophilia, (2) honestly define their positions on a continuum regarding attitudes toward homosexuality, using the anonymous Bead Box.

Materials

Note card sets for each group of 6-8 students; bead box

Time

30-45 minutes, depending on time spent processing

Procedures

Prior to the session, print the following statements on several sets of 5 x 7 index cards. Explain to the group that many people unknowingly and knowingly contribute to homophobia in our culture. This activity is a card-sorting activity designed to gain understanding of biases toward and against homosexuality. Show the continuum and define homophobia and hemophilia on the extremes. Divide the class into groups of 6-8. Give each group a packet of the well shuffled card statements below. Have them align their set of cards from what they believe to be the <u>least</u> homophobia attitudes/behaviors to most homophobic attitudes/behaviors. If they believe any are equal, they can align them in the same place on the continuum. After about 1 5 minutes, have groups walk around and compare their sequences, speculating why other groups placed certain cards in certain orders. Discuss the alignments as a total group.

<u>Statements:</u>   (adapted from <u>Lesbian and Gay issues</u>)

1. You stop yourself from doing/saying certain things because someone might think you are gay or lesbian.

2. You believe gays or lesbians can influence others to become homosexual, especially children.

3. You believe gays and lesbians should be barred from certain positions or professions (clergy, day care, military).

4. You intentionally do/say things so that people will know you are <u>not</u> gay or lesbian.

5. You would avoid a physician, psychologist, physical therapist or other health professional you knew/believed to be gay or lesbian.

6. You believe AIDS is a punishment against homosexuals for evil behavior.

7. You would attend a gay or lesbian bar, march, rally or sponsored event.

8. You would wear a button that says " How dare you assume that I am heterosexual?"

9. You can identify three positive aspects of a gay or lesbian relationship and three negative aspects of a heterosexual relationship, and vice versa.

10. You laugh at "queer" jokes.

11. You would go to a gay or lesbian bar, march or rally to heckle or assault participants.

12. You would object to your next door neighbors being a gay or lesbian couple.

13. You tell "queer" jokes.

After processing the sequential order of the cards, present the group with the following continuum of attitudes toward homosexuality, and explain each position. Relate them to the order of the statements. Using the bead box (student privately drops the color of bead into small box that represents his/her true feelings about homosexuality), have students anonymously identify their own attitudes toward gays and lesbians. Open the bead box, count the beads and show the results to the group.

To close, have students complete a "Today I learned..." and "Being a gay or lesbian person...". Collect the papers before students leave. Read selected observations as a review at the start of next class period if used in a standard class.

Homophobia   Homophilia

Dirty/pervert	Disease	Tolerance	Support	Advocacy	Practice
(Blue)	(Green)	(Red)	(White)	(Orange)	(Yellow)

Handling Hot Emotions in the Classroom

Because the subject of homosexuality can bring out serious prejudices and reactions, instructors need to be able to intervene with a stabilizing process. Should there be a heated exchange between two people, you can engage the following sequence:

1. Call "time out" and use the referee hand signal for "time-out" while moving toward the antagonists. Remind the class about respecting others' rights to their own opinions and beliefs, whether we agree with them or not.

2. Ask the two people in conflict to face each other so that they can make eye contact. ("Jane, I'd like you and Mark to face each other...")

3. Ask student A to listen carefully, while student B tells him/her what he/she wants to say, without interrupting. ('Mark, I'd like for you to listen carefully while Jane...")

4. After student B has finished, ask student A to repeat back the major idea(s) of student B, and start by saying, " You're saying..." ("Mark, I'd like for you to summarize what Jane just expressed, starting with 'You're saying that...'")

5. Repeat the process with student A putting out his/her position, without **interruption,** and afterwards, student B repeats back student A's opinions by starting with, "You believe... or you are saying..."

6. Next, student B says, "When I hear your position, I fee....because .... I wish you ....

7. Student A repeats back I understand that you feel ..,because... ; You wish I.......

8. Reverse the process. Student A says "When I hear your position, I feel ....because .... ; I wish you....

9. Student B repeats back, " I understand that you feel....because...; You wish I.....

10. Return to the session plan at this point.

Note: A cue card on poster board with the communication cues is helpful to achieve this two-cycle communication exchange.

If a student becomes testy and refuses to cooperate in this exercise, ask students if they agree or disagree with the dissident's position, using the marble box. They drop a green marble for a AGREE response; a red marble for a DISAGREE response; or a yellow marble for a "PASS" response. Students, as a whole, usually support a moderate or compassionate position in such situations.

If verbal or physical abuse ensues, discharge the student(s) from the session, and file a record of the incident with student affairs or the appropriate officer. Have two students sign as witnesses to the event as you have recorded it. You may also file a grievance with the appropriate committee on campus.

A final note of caution. These activities are intended to be presented by leaders who are both comfortable with their own sexuality and comfortable in acceptance of/ advocacy for GLB. Before committing to a session, presenters should complete the activities themselves, examining their motives and being clear about their values regarding homosexuality. Persons charged with securing trainers or training trainers would do well to administer attitudinal assessments and evaluate videotaped practice sessions prior to having trainers work with students. Success mostly depends on the skills, attitude and role modeling of an effective instructor.

30

The Sexual Activity Survey

Submitted by Randall R. Cottrell, D.Ed., CHES
University of Cincinnati, Cincinnati, OH

The sexual activity survey was designed for use in a college level personal health or human sexuality class. It may also be useful, however, in certain other large group presentations or group counseling sessions offered by a student health center. The idea for this activity originated with a student some 15 years ago. Essentially the student was interested in determining the extent to which his classmates participated in the various sexual activities presented in the textbook and discussed in class. It was his observation that many students developed a somewhat polarized and unfounded belief that either everyone was participating in a particular sexual behavior or no one was participating in a particular sexual behavior. He suggested conducting an anonymous sexual behavior survey in class. The following activity has evolved from his suggestion.

Objectives

Upon completion of this activity, the students will be able to:

1. Discuss the range of sexual behaviors reported by students in their class.

2. Compare and contrast the sexual behaviors of their class with those of previous classes.

3. Develop summary statements related to the following:

    a. What was learned from the activity.

    b. What surprises resulted from the activity.

    c. What questions arose as a result of the activity.

Materials

Two 8 1/2 x I I inch sheets of blank paper per student.
Four large pieces of newsprint
Adhesive tape
Four large point, dark colored marking pens
Extra pencils

Pre-Activity Information and Instructions

This activity is typically conducted near the end of the term so that students and faculty have had time to establish a good rapport. A brief preview of the activity is presented to students during the class period prior to actually conducting the Sexual Survey Activity. Originally this was done to provide advanced warning to students who might be uncomfortable with such an activity. In actuality, the preview seems to elevate student interest and attendance is typically near 100% for the day of the activity.

It is important to set the stage for the activity prior to starting. Students are told that the purpose of the Sexual Survey Activityi is to provide them with an awareness of the range of sexual behaviors in which fellow classmates and previous students enrolled in the same course have participated. As part of the pre-activity instructions to students, it is stressed that there are no "right" or "wrong" behaviors. Simply because the majority of students may have participated in a particular behavior does not make that behavior "right" or "good" or "acceptable." Conversely, when only one or very few students have participated in a behavior, the behavior is not "wrong" or "bad" or "unacceptable." The intent of the activity is not to encourage students to alter their sexual behaviors or to conform with those of their classmates; it is to raise student awareness as to the range of sexual behaviors and practices within the current group.

Students are also cautioned against generalizing the findings from this activity to that of all college students. Since enrollment in the course on our campus is primarily comprised of health education majors and non-majors taking the class for elective credit, the results may not be representative of the entire student body.

Directions and Set-up

A stack of blank 8 1/2 x I I inch paper is circulated around the room and each student is instructed to take two sheets (Large note cards can also be used). Students are then instructed to fold both sheets of paper in half and tear them in two so they now have four half sheets of paper.

Each half sheet is labeled at the top as Card 1, Card 2, Card 3 or Card 4. If the class has a fairly even number of male and female students, the cards can also be marked with a 'M' or 'F' identifier at the top to depict gender. This allows for separate male and female results. If there are either a small number of males or females in the class, the gender identifier should not be used as it may compromise the anonymity of individuals in the smaller group. For example, if there were only four males in the class and all four had participated in oraf sex, their anonymity- would have been lost. There must be enough students in a group to be reasonably sure of varied responses to the questions.

Students are instructed that they may only write on the cards with pencils or black ink pens. This prevents loss of anonymity for students that may write with non-traditional colored ink such as green or purple. Extra pencils are made available for students that may not have an appropriate writing instrument. Students are also encouraged to move their desks or chairs around the room until they feel comfortable that no other students can see their answers.

At this point students are told they are going to be asked a number of personal questions regarding their sexual behaviors stressing that their responses will be totally anonymous. They are encouraged to answer as honestly as possible. Any student not wishing to participate is given the option of either leaving the room or remaining in the room and submitting blank cards.

Starting with question 1 on Card 1, each question is read by the instructor to the students (see Figures 1-4). When the questions on all four cards have been read, students are given the opportunity to suggest additional questions they may wish to have answered during the activity and these responses are placed on the back of card four (often these additional questions are added to the activity the next time it is used). A specific location in the room is designated for each of the four cards to be deposited. Students must physically get up from their seats and distribute their cards to these designated locations. Once this is completed the students divide themselves evenly among the four locations and work together to tabulate the results for each question from all collected cards. A sample tabulation from a previous class or one developed by the instructor can be used to guide students in this process. A volunteer from each group clearly writes the results on newsprint using the large point marker. The four large sheets of newsprint are then hung in front of the room. An example of a tabulated card for a group with no gender distinction can be seen in Figure 5 and for a group with gender distinction in Figure 6.

With the tabulated results displayed in front of the room, the instructor repeats each question and reads the results. Over time the instructor may accumulate an ongoing record of results from previous classes. These results can be presented and compared to those of the current class as an added point of reference. During this reporting of results, students are encouraged to ask questions and make comments. After the results of all four cards have been reported, students are asked to complete the following three sentence stems on a clean sheet of paper: 1) From this activity I learned that.... 2) From this activity I was surprised that.... 3) As a result of this activity I want to know.... The completed sentences are collected and reviewed by the instructor.

The activity often sparks lively discussions and identifies areas of student need or interest that can be covered in future classes. Many students entering the course know of the sexual behavior activity and eagerly await the day when it will occur. Comments on post-course student evaluations consistently identify this activity as a course highlight.

Figure I. CARD 1 QUESTIONS

1. Are you married, engaged, single and going steady, or single unattached?
2. Have you ever had sexual intercourse?
3. Are you now having sexual intercourse on a regular basis?
4. At what age did you first have sexual intercourse?
5. Have you ever had a "one night stand?"
6. Would you describe your sex life as more spontaneous or relationship oriented?
7. Have you ever participated in what you would described as "Kinky Sex?" If yes, please   explain the behavior or situation.

Figure 2: Card 2 Questions

1. Have you ever been physically raped? If yes was it date rape or an unknown attacker?
2. Have you ever been psychologically raped? (felt coerced to have sex with someone when you did not want to - i.e. boyfriend says the relationship is over unless... or boss says no promotion unless ...)
3. Are you now or have you ever been involved in an incestual relationship?
4. Have you ever had sex with someone where there was an age difference of five or more years? If so, was this relationship with someone five years older? five years younger? Or relationships with persons both five years older and five years younger?
5. Have you ever masturbated?
6. Do you masturbate regularly?
7. Have you ever participated in masturbation activities while in the presence of an individual of the opposite sex? of the same sex?

Figure 3: Card 3 Questions

1. Do you currently use contraception 100% of the time when having sex?
2. In the past have you used contraception 100% of the time when having sex?
3. What type of contraception have you used the most in your sexual relationships?
4. Have you ever been involved in an unwanted pregnancy? (This includes being pregnant for females and fathering an unwanted pregnancy for males)
5. Have you ever had an abortion? (For males has a pregnant partner ever had an abortion?)
6. Have you ever participated in bestiality (sexual involvement with an animal)
7. In your sexual relationships would you consider yourself to be the passive partner, aggressive partner or an equal partner?
8. Have you ever been diagnosed with a sexually transmitted disease? If so, what STD did you have?
9. Have you ever been approached by a teacher, employer or professor to have sex? If so, did you have sex with that person?

Figure 4: Card 4 Questions

1. Have you seen hard core pornography other than as an assignment for this course?
2. Do you consider yourself to be primarily a heterosexual, homosexual or bisexual?
3. Have your ever had a homosexual experience.
4. Have you ever skinny dipped with members of the opposite sex since childhood.
5. Have you ever explicitly paid for sex?
6. Have you ever explicitly been paid for having sex?
7. Have you ever participated in group sex? (three or more individuals at the same time)
8. Have you ever participated in anal sex?
9. What is the total number of sexual partners you have had to this point in time?
10. Up to this point in time, have you altered your persona sexual behaviors as a result of the HIV/AIDS epidemic? If so, how?

Figure 5: Card 1 Results

1. Married - 4; Engaged - 7; Single - 29;
   Single attached - *15;* Single unattached - 14.

2. Yes - 31 No - 9

3. Yes - 27 No -13

4.

5 - I	10 - 0	*15 -* 3	20 - 2
6 - 0	11 - 1	16 - 9	26 - 1
7 - 0	12 - 0	17 - 4	33 - 1
8 - 0	13 - 2	18 - 1	NA-9
9 - 0	14 - 2	19 - 4	

5. Yes - 14 ; No-17; NA-9

6. Spontaneous - 6; Relationship - 25; NA-9

7. Yes - *5;* Bondage - 3; No-26 S&M-1
   NA-9 Kitchen Table - I

Figure 6: Card 2 Results

	Female	Male
1.	Yes - I No-15 NA-6	Yes - 0 No-15 NA-3
2.	Yes - 8 No-8 NA-6	Yes - 2 No-13 NA-3
3.	Yes - I No-15 NA-6	Yes - 0 No-15 NA-3
4.	Yes - 6 No-10 NA-6 > 5 years - *5* < 5 years - I Both - 0	Yes - 3 No-12 NA-3 > 5 years - 1 < 5 years - I Both - 1
5.	Yes - 17 No-5	Yes - 16 No-2
6.	Yes - *15* No-7	Yes - 13 No-5
7.	Cross Sex - *5* Same Sex - 3 Both - 0 Neither - 9	Cross Sex - 4 Same Sex - I Both - 0 Neither - I I

Exercises in Understanding Human Sexuality

Submitted by Lorie L. Dewald, Ed.D., ATC, CHES
Shippensburg University, Shippensburg, PA

In an attempt to assist my students in understanding differences in human lives and sexuality, I developed these activities to put students into the daily living situations of people with heterosexual and homosexual lifestyles.

Objectives

1. The student will develop a better understanding for the complexities and simplicities of human relationships.

2. The student will experience the impact of one's sexuality on daily living.

Materials

Time

1-3 class periods and time outside the classroom (1-2 hours).

Activity Introduction

Our society is comprised of people with various occupations, educational levels, family structures, ethnic backgrounds, religions, and sexual orientations. These and many other influences can significantly affect the communication within family structures. Modern technology has taken our world well into the next century. But, despite the advances, our society is still entrenched in the behaviors of past decades when the topic of sexuality and its development are considered. Controversy still exists in our society with regards to whose responsibility it is to teach the subject of sexuality to our children. The teaching of sexuality is receiving more attention as our society addresses potentially life-threatening infections and diseases spread through sexual relations between people and their partners. The following suggestions are made to assist educators in their personal understanding and considerations of their own biases and cultural influences toward alternative lifestyle choices found within our society.

Suggestions

The characteristics found within the members of our culture are used to place people with like characteristics into categories. Sometimes these preestablished categories have a negative impact upon the individual who is been placed in the category by other members of our society. Rarely, do we (as individuals) place ourselves in these categories, but rather we are singled out and put in these groupings by others. The personal costs can sometimes be very high. One frequent way in which judgments are passed and categorizations made are based upon visual observations (i.e., skin color, hair color, eye color, gender, glasses, orthodontic appliances, mannerisms).

Recently, our society has become increasingly more interested in categorizing people into sexual orientations or the preconceived ideas of a person's sexual orientation. Immense consequences can result from these categorizations, many of which are permanent. It is increasingly more popular to judge people in this way, and it is apparent that we are losing touch with the bottom-line facts in sexuality. We must only simply recall Maslow's Hierarchy of Needs to begin this greater understanding of people's uniqueness. One of Maslow's hierarchy of needs is to "give and receive love." Based upon this premise, I encourage health educators to reevaluate their teaching of sexuality and consider this idea: when two people are loving one another, they are simply attempting to satisfy one of their innate needs — the giving and receiving of love. The consequences of this consideration can be a more promising acceptance of people and their varying choices of the individuals with whom they have chosen to love and fulfill their needs (regardless of the gender similarities or differences of the two people who are loving one another).

Exercises

The following exercises were developed in order to raise the consciousness of college students towards the real differences within the lifestyle alternatives found within our culture.

The exercises are done individually and with a partner. The partner experiences are of two types: (1) with an opposite gender partner, and (2) with a partner of the same gender. The partner exercises are to be compared with one another, i.e., gender different (heterosexual) and gender same (homosexual) partnerships. The reason for these comparisons is so the student will be able to recognize the societal actions and reactions to the different couples.

Following the completion of each exercise, the student is to write a "personal reflection paper." "The personal reflection paper' is <u>not a research paper</u>. It is a paper that is an open sharing of their thoughts, feelings, insight, and foresight into the experience they had while completing the assignment. The paper is of a length that allows the student to share the scope of the full meaning of the assignment through the student's eyes and life considerations. The "personal reflection papers" are kept confidential with the instructor and are returned to the student upon the instructor's reading. Grades <u>are not</u> to be given to the "personal reflection papers," only a check off that the assignment was completed. The "personal reflection paper" must be double spaced, and of a length that is an appropriate gesture of the students' experience with the assignment. The experiences are to be completed throughout the semester. (A recommendation might be one per week.)

Observe people's responses, reactions, etc. to each of these exercises and experiences. The students are encouraged to talk with ones partner following each of these exercises about the feelings they had while completing them.

Individual Activities

1. What would one's family's reactions be to the acknowledgment to them of one's sexual choice in partners?

2. Self reflect upon the potential consequences that one might encounter from the silence of not communicating to one's family about the person who is mutually loving them in their life.

3. What are the rules in ones state that govern the wills, living wills, and life insurance benefits of same gender and opposite gender partners? Do the rules change if the partners are married or living together?

4. What religious bodies approve and disapprove of alternative lifestyle choices. Discuss with a member of the clergy the issue of sexuality. How does one's own religious belief influence one's personal sexuality?

5. Shop for a special occasion card for a same gender and opposite gender partner. (i.e., birthday, anniversary, holiday, etc.)

6. Go to the library and listen to the audiotapes on reserve. After listening to the songs, determine which one is male gender specific, female gender specific, gay specific, lesbian specific, and heterosexual specific. The purpose of this is to show the students that music exists for all people within our society.

7. Go into any music store and look for such artists as:

   If these are not found, ask a sales person where they might be located or if another music store might have them available.

8. Find and visit a specialty bookstore that caters to a gender specific population and alternative lifestyle choice population.

9. Find and experience social settings where people meet others of like preference (i.e. bars).

Partner Activities

10. Investigate the renting of a one-bedroom apartment with a male and then a female partner.

11. Pursue the securing of a marriage license or partnership registration in the county/state in which you live.

12. Pursue the opening of joint bank accounts together.

13. Pursue the establishing of insurance (life, health, auto, etc.) together.

14. See a physician or health care provider and disclose to them your sexual preference.

15. Walk on campus (during peak hours) holding hands with both same-gender and opposite-gender partners.

16. How do you plan on introducing your partner to other people (i.e. husband, wife, lover, significant other, spouse, partner, etc.) Next, introduce each other to another person on campus. What is their reaction?

17. Spend 24 hours not touching another human being in public.

18. Spend 24 hours not touching another human being in private.

Brief Description of the Evaluation Techniques

Instructor's Recommendation   A follow-up suggestion to the student assignments is to promote in-class discussion on the experiences. Assemble the students into small groups (males and females separate) to talk about the feelings **they** had before, during, and after the exercises. Next assemble the two groups together in a full class discussion to share the similarities and differences of their experiences with one another. Suggest the class brainstorm solutions or personal actions that they can take to address the problems that they have identified.

NOTE: The suggestions shared in this teaching idea have proven to be very powerful activities and have been very successfully incorporated into sexuality classes taught by this author and student comments unanimously have encouraged their continued usage. Based upon these developments, I recommend others to try them as well.

Teaching The Concept of Sexual Readiness

Submitted by Lin S. Fox, M.S.W., Ed.D.
Kean College of New Jersey, Union, NJ

Preparing young people for their sexual futures is the responsibility of parents as well as adults from various institutions. As educators we are most aware of young people's quest to determine when they are ready for sex. At issue is not a specific age to have sexual intercourse but, rather, why it may be best to abstain from sexual intercourse, and under what conditions to agree to sexual intercourse. These are the issues of "sexual readiness." Convincing one's self that he or she is ready ought not to take place in an awkward or impulsive few moments.

Various questions need to be considered. However, such questions are not at the forefront of most adolescents' imaginations. We must help teens ruminate on the decision that will have lasting personal effects. The task of conceptualizing the issues that contribute to sexual readiness can be accomplished in the classroom.

Objectives

When educators have completed this activity students will:

1. be made aware of crucial issues regarding the readiness for sexual intercourse,

2. know better the value of discussing these issues with a partner, and

3. have a clearer understanding of the potential consequences of one's sex-related decisions and behaviors.

Materials

paper/pens
chalkboard/chalk

Time

45 minutes, or more

Procedure

Tell the class that today they are going to work together to come to an understanding of what it means to be ready for sexual intercourse.

Divide the class into groups of no more than 5, making sure to have both males and females creating a balance of opinion based on gender.

Explain that they will work in the small groups and then report to the larger group.

Describe the following situation: "You are sitting around talking with your favorite younger, 15 year old cousin. The cousin looks up to you and values your opinion especially on things controversial. You cousin tells you he/she has been going out regularly with a boy/girlfriend and making out is hot and heavy. In fact, they'll probably 'do it' next time they're together. What do you think?"

Ask the students to collectively come up with responses within this framework: What do you want to tell your cousin who believes you know more about sex and relationships than he/she does? What do you want to tell your cousin to think about before agreeing to have sexual intercourse? Remember that you want to be helpful and protective. Make a list and be ready to explain why the issue is important.

Allow about 20 minutes for the groups to generate a spectrum of ideas.

Give each small group a chance to tell one of their ideas allowing for larger group reaction and participation. Go around each group in turn until significant factors that explore for sexual readiness have been listed and discussed. They will soon see that a lot of teen relationships cannot pass this analysis.

The following suggested content areas are representative of "sexual readiness." Guide students through them as they describe what they would ask their cousins.

1. Actual Feelings for Each Other - How would they describe these feelings? Is it love, and does it matter? Lies and lines may be tossed around to mask actual or uncertain feelings between adolescents. Do they understand commitment or are they pursuing adventure, or succumbing to sexual intimidation? A serious discussion about "love" and its meanings may take off.

2. Pressure Behind Feelings- From where come these feelings of pressure to have sexual intercourse? Do they understand the power of biology to satisfy physical yearnings? Are they moved by what their friends are doing sexually, and don't want to be left behind? What do they really think about necking and petting instead of full intercourse? Figure out with them how they can come to value nonintercourse sexual expression despite wanting to play out MTV images of "grown up" sex.

3. Birth Control Types - To what extent are they paying attention to birth control? Who will use what? Who will obtain and pay for a mutually agreed upon birth control method? Biologically we are set up to want another person sexually - nature's plan is to see to it that a certain amount of human species reproduction gets done, whether we think about it much, or not. Earnestly reflect with

them why the hard part, especially for the young, is making a conscious effort to avoid conception until it makes sense as a goal.

4. Birth Control Failure - What if the birth control fails? Are they aware of what their options are if pregnancy occurs? Who will handle the costs financially? Have them consider the cost of personal feelings over having created an unplanned pregnancy, ending a pregnancy, or giving up a baby? Further, question together the kind of resources necessary to adequately raise a child as an unwed parent?

5. Sexually Transmitted Diseases - Are they aware of how easy it is to pass on a sexually transmittable disease? Explain that even the nicest people get and give STDs of which one of the many can kill. Do they know where to go for treatment? Discuss some of the more recent STDs entering this country. Note the limitations of medical professionals to halt disease progression.,

6. Sexual Guilt - Have they considered how they will feel about themselves after participating in intercourse? Everything changes after the "first time". Guilt is a special form of regret. Even in the highly charged sexual atmosphere of adolescence, parental and religious teachings are not forgotten. Do they understand how a loss of self-respect is interconnected with loss of self-esteem?

7. Reputation - What about character and reputation should others find out about their sexual activities? Adolescents can be mean. Rumors abound. Do they understand what a double standard is? Explain that this decidedly biased concept against females had heftyconsequences in the 1950s and still does in the 1990s within many social groups.

8. Relationships End - What if the relationship ends after participating in intercourse? A ruined relationship can leave a young person with feelings of betrayal, shaken trust, and even fear of commitment. Do they realize that when a relationship breaks up the wounds are almost always deeper when sexual intercourse was part of the experience?

9. Sexual Manners - If the decision is still to pursue sexual intercourse, have they considered where? Creating a private atmosphere is an indication of caring and maturity; drunk and in the back seat of a car is not. Manners, sexual and otherwise, in an evolving relationship need to be discussed, even demonstrated. Further, do they understand when pursuit becomes date rape?

10. Misleading Expectations - What kinds of expectations do they have about sexual intercourse? Impressions can be misleading. Are they aware of the performance anxieties felt by most people at first intercourse? Do they know that many females do not have

orgasms in their early experiences with intercourse, unlike the experience for most males? Include some of the problems that result especially from alcohol use. Sex looks so much better, easier, and more fun in media presentations than often occurs in reality.

If time permits, elicit discussion directed to the normalization of "partial abstinence" - nonintercourse sexual pleasure. Ask "what is the chance that a ninth grader will be ready to handle the above concerns?" Most will agree that it is not likely, admitting the value of discussing abstaining from intercourse itself for the time being.

Teaching young people to recognize situations that can lead to sexual pressure and practicing to say "no" and /or "not now" are possible extensions to this lesson.

Evaluation

Techniques to determine effectiveness of teaching tool include:

1. a spontaneous role play of the older/younger cousin situation, and

2. content-based exam questions.

33

Birth Control

Submitted by Wendy Kyman, Ph.D.
CUNY/Barauch College, New York, NY

Birth control is an essential topic of discussion. Many sexually active individuals/couples do not use contraceptive devices/methods. Perhaps as many as 50% of pregnancies to American couples are unplanned and the rate of adolescent pregnancy is alarmingly high. This lesson is aimed at presenting correct information concerning contraception and contraceptive devices/methods, as well as fostering students' decision-making and responsibility-taking skills, by encouraging them to establish general as well as personal criteria for selecting contraceptives.

Objectives

1. List and detail reasons why people do not use birth control.

2. Distinguish between contraception-related myths/misconceptions and correct information.

3. Establish criteria for choosing a birth control device/method.

4. Describe and present various birth control devices.

5. Explain how devices/methods are used, theoretical and user effectiveness of each, and advantages and disadvantages of each.

6. Discuss ways to make birth control use a "shared responsibility."

7. Identify influences on contraceptive decision-making.

8. Outline historical background as well as future directions in contraception and contraceptives.

Materials

Materials necessary: birth control kit - including condom/spermicide, birth control pills, diaphragm, cervical cap; IUD; Norplant (if possible); visual aids - large graphics of vasectomy, tubal ligation.

Time

Approximately 2 1/2 hours is needed to successfully complete this lesson. This is adequate time for presenting the material, discussion, and evaluation.

Procedure

The class is organized in typical college setting. Male and female students are situated in seats. Most students are in their early 20's. The lesson begins with a discussion of adolescent pregnancies and the problems inherent in this situation - medical, social, economic, etc. This leads to a discussion of unintended pregnancies among all age groups and reasons why people do not use birth control methods/devices such as: lack of correct information; lack of decision-making skills; using birth control requires planning and forethought and some people refuse to admit and take responsibility for sexual activity; interferes with spontaneity; fear of potential side effects.

Discussion then is directed towards taking responsibility for sexual activity and developing decision-making skills. Students are asked to assess their attitudes about contraception and determine what factors influence their choices regarding contraception. (There is never the assumption that students are currently sexually active.) Also special consideration is given to those students whose religions/cultural beliefs preclude the use of contraceptive devices.

The lesson now turns to specific contraceptive devices. One by one each device is displayed including a condom-use demonstration (using instructor's fingers). As each device is displayed and available for students' to view (and later to examine more fully) the device is described, use and effectiveness explained and then the instructor elicits from students the advantages and disadvantages of each device. After the devices are described, the methods, withdrawal, sterilization, etc. are discussed in the same way. Students then individually establish criteria which will enable them to evaluate each method/device and select one/ several.

Students' questions and opinions are encouraged throughout the lesson.

Evaluation Techniques

The traditional evaluation technique of objective exams is useful for the cognitive aspect of this lesson.

For the affective/behavioral components students can:

1. Complete a pre-post lesson questionnaire to determine which, if any, attitudinal and behavioral changes occurred. Questions such as: Will you use contraceptives? Why? Why not? Which method will you use? Why?

2. Keep a journal of attitudinal/behavioral changes.

3. Visit and evaluate family planning agencies.

34

Pregnancy and Childbirth

Submitted by Wendy Kyman, Ph.D.
Baruch College, The City University of New York, NY

The overwhelming majority of students will become parents. Therefore students must be cognizant of the factors involved in this momentous, life-changing event. Many decisions are required concerning childbearing in general and also specific decisions must be made at each stage of the process. In addition, new advances in technologies often evoke ethical concerns.

Objectives

1. List and determine reasons why people choose to have children (or choose not to have children).

2. Distinguish between childbearing related myths/misconceptions and correct information.

3. Outline historical/cross-cultural perspectives as well as future directions in childbearing.

4. Trace and describe the childbearing process from pre-conception to post partum.

5. Identify signs associated with each stage of the process.

6. Identify decisions required of each stage of the process.

7. Discuss ways in which childbearing is "shared responsibility."

Materials

Visual aids - large graphics depicting the stages of childbearing from conception through childbirth: video - (choose from several available) on actual labor and childbirth.

Time

Approximately 2 1/2 hours is needed to successfully complete this lesson. This is adequate time for presenting the material, discussion and evaluation.

Procedure

The class is organized in a typical college setting. Male and female students are situated in seats. Most students are in their early 20s. This lesson is focused on developing decision making skills concerning childbearing.

The lesson begins with the instructor asking students to raise their hands if they plan to have children (most do). The instructor then asks those students "why'" (most are shocked by this question). This leads to a discussion of societal/family/personal expectations to have children. Most students have given very little thought to why they will become parents and the reality of what is involved in parenting. The discussion also is directed at feelings and thoughts about individuals who choose not to have children and those who are unable to have children. The class also discusses family planning: the number of children they want, the spacing between each child, and when they will begin to have children (specific age, number of years in relationship, specific point in career).

The instructor then draws a line on the board representing the childbearing process.

pre-conception - conception -	prenatal	- childbirth - post partum
	<1 2 3> <4 5 6>	<7 8 9>
	1st 2nd	3rd
	trimester trimester	trimester

Each stage in the process is discussed, focusing on the signs which accompany each stage and the decisions which are required of each stage, e.g., decisions, life-style changes, choosing health provider, birth location, childbirth education program, having diagnostic procedures, etc. Signs: fatigue, missed period, appetite changes, etc.

Childbirth is discussed in detail and the specifics of labor and delivery are provided, as well as the decisions required, e.g., interventions, pain relieving medications, fetal heart monitor; support people, breathing and relaxation.

Next, post partum decisions are detailed such as: breast/bottle feed, child care responsibilities, return to work, spacing of next child. The lesson will also include discussion of infertility, miscarriages, premature births as well as alternative ways of parenting, surrogate parenthood, frozen embryos, IVF, alternative insemination.

Evaluation Techniques

The traditional evaluation technique of objective exam is useful for the cognitive aspect of this lesson.

112

For the affective/behavioral components students can:

1. Write a reaction paper concerning feelings and attitudes after viewing the childbirth video.

2. Interview relatives/friends about their parenting/childbirth experiences.

3. Visit an alternative birthing center and evaluate the agency in terms of objective and subjective criteria.

4. Research advances in technology and discuss personal feelings about these methods.

35

He Asks, She Says and She Asks, He Says
Submitted by Mark A. Temple, Ph.D., CHES
Texas Tech University, Lubbock, TX

Students often claim that they do not understand the "opposite sex." This activity provides each student a chance to become actively involved in the learning process. It creates a nonthreatening, nonjudgmental, culturally sensitive forum in which students can ask those questions which they have always wanted answered.

Objectives

1. The learner will be able to cite similarities and differences in male and female responses.

2. The learner will become aware of similarities and differences in the cognitive and affective processes of men and women.

3. The learner will evaluate his or her own perception of members of the opposite sex.

Materials

This is a simple activity. The students will need to submit questions in some form or fashion. The only materials are paper and writing utensil.

Time

Students will need a deadline for submission of questions. I allow one class meeting for the actual activity. Both females and males have about 25 minutes each to answer questions. The activity could obviously take longer if more time is available.

Description of Activity

I present this activity during the relationships' section of a human sexuality course. It would also fit well in a section related to gender differences or issues. Before the actual activity, I explain to the class that they will have an opportunity to ask the opposite sex questions. Students submit questions to me before the lesson. I review each question and compile a general list. The instructor may add questions if he or she would like to see other areas covered during the activity. At the class meeting immediately preceding the activity, I pass out a compilation of questions. Each student receives a list of both male and female questions. I ask the students to review each question and consider how he or she might respond. On the day of the activity, I divide the class by gender. Males move to one side of the room and face their female classmates. I begin the activity by asking the female students which question they would like answered first. Once students make a selection, I present that question to the males. One or more males respond to the question. Repeat the activity in alternating fashion until the class period is complete. The instructor ensures the inclusion of all students in the process. Do not allow one student or a few students to monopolize the discussion. Also, the teacher has a duty to promote any diversity present. I will often ask specific students if they would like to respond to an item.

Evaluation

I evaluate this activity through student reaction papers. Each student submits a paper explaining his or her reaction to the activity and what he or she learned. The student includes his or her understanding of similarities and differences in responses. He or she also submits his or her own perception of members of the opposite based on this activity. Student response has always been favorable. Most students express the sentiment that not only did they enjoy the activity but learned a great deal. They commonly express that they feel more comfortable communicating with members of the opposite sex.

36

Gender Benders
Submitted by Christine Beyer, Ph.D.
North Carolina Central University, Durham, NC

Gender stereotyping is harmful because it limits individual choice and opportunity. This activity has value in enabling students to assess gender bias as evidenced in themselves and as evidenced in others.

Educational Objective
Students test their levels of gender stereotyping.

Grade Level   College/High School

Content/Methods
The facilitator reads the scenario entitled, "A Day At The Beach." The characters in the story are intentionally given the generic names: Terry, Tracy, Chris, Pat, Lee, Coach Martin and Dr. Maverick. Students are asked to rank the characters in the scenario giving a ranking of 1 to a character they most respected to a score of 7 for the person they least respected. Students are placed in three groups. One student group should be all female, another group all male and the third group mixed gender. Each group must compromise and agree on one group ranking of the characters. Students record their rankings on the chalkboard.

> ### "A Day At The Beach"
> Terry's parents have a beach house. Terry's parents would be out of town for the weekend. Terry thought that it would be a perfect time to plan a drinking party at the beach house. Terry was under age and could not purchase liquor. Terry asked a stranger at the liquor store, named Pat, to purchase the liquor. Pat purchased the liquor for Terry, charging a twenty dollar service charge. Coach Martin was outside the liquor store watching the entire transaction and chose to ignore it. Terry, Lee and Chris went to the beech house and began drinking. Chris spiked Lee's drink with the intention of encouraging sexual activity. Lee became gravely ill from excessive alcohol. Chris called Dr. Maverick for help. Dr. Maverick called both 911 and Terry's parents.

Evaluation

Discussion of the rationale for group and individual rankings follows. The instructor should emphasize that the gender of each character was never identified. The instructor facilitates discussion about assumptions made concerning the gender of each character.

37

Enhancing Self-esteem Through Peer Interaction

Submitted by Dawn Larsen, Ph.D., CHES
Mankato State University, Mankato, MN

Adolescents' experiences of growing up have changed dramatically over the last several decades. They spend at least 40 percent of their waking hours out of school, and must decide what to do with their time. These decisions involve both risk and responsibility. For many, the out-of-school hours present risks for substance abuse, crime, violence, and sexual activity which can lead to unplanned pregnancy and sexually transmitted diseases. For others, they provide a chance to play sports, interact with friends, and explore new challenges. Sound decision-making reflects the personal and social competence of teens and is often directly influenced by their self-esteem. Unfortunately, adolescence is the time during which self-esteem is likely to drop considerably. The following activity is designed to promote or encourage positive self-esteem among participants. Though designed for adolescents, it can be used successfully in groups ranging in age from middle school through adults.

Objectives

1. Participants will discuss characteristics they admire and respect in themselves.

2. Students will discuss qualities they admire and respect in others.

3. Students will recognize the power of praise and self-appraisal in promoting and maintaining self-esteem.

Grade Level   Middle school through adult.

Materials

Bag of M & M candies
Small paper cups
3 x 5 cards
Pencils

Time

40-50 minutes

Methods

Students are divided into small groups of 4-5 people. Each is given a small paper cup containing a portion of M & M candies, a card, and a pencil. (Be sure all colors of the candies are in each cup.) Students are told they cannot eat the candies until the conclusion of the exercise. Candies are divided into colors. For each M & M of the following color they write on their cards:

Red: A compliment directed at another group member.

Yellow: A quality they admire in themselves.

Orange: A characteristic they admire in a friend.

Green: A reason why people respect them.

Brown: An accomplishment they are proud of.

Blue: A goal they have set for the future.

They must write at least one entry for each color. (Entries should target specific qualities—simply saying "I'm nice" or "He's a good friend" is not appropriate). After about 15-20 minutes, students stop and share what is written on their cards. As they share each entry they may eat one of the candies. Each member summarizes and describes a reaction to this experience.

Questions to Address

1. Was it difficult to think of positive characteristics about yourself? Why?

2. Was it easier to think of positive characteristics in others? Why or why not?

3. Did you feel comfortable or uncomfortable receiving compliments from others? Why?

4. Have you learned anything new or different about yourself?

Suggested alternatives to M & M candies include: dried fruits of different colors, different types of pretzels, different types of nuts, and a variety of fresh fruits and raw vegetables.

38

Stress Reactivity

Submitted by Roseann M. Lyle, Ph.D., FACSM
Purdue University, West Lafayette, IN

Cardiovascular disease (CVD) is the leading cause of death in the US. While there is some controversy over the relationship between a person's stress level and risk of CVD, many believe that repeated episodes of acute stress and/or chronic stress may directly or indirectly increase risk of CVD. For example, a full blown stress reaction can release a variety of biochemicals into the circulation which increase blood pressure and serum cholesterol levels.

Some people , who tend to have a greater reaction to a stressful situation than others, have been referred to as "hot reactors" and may be especially vulnerable. Most people do not realize how quickly homeostasis can be upset by stress. Nor do they realize that stressors arising from both the mind and the body can rapidly induce physiological arousal. This activity demonstrates how blood pressure and heart rate respond to a mental stressor and two different types of physical stressors and provides the opportunity to discuss factors that may be related to the variability in the level of reactivity observed among different people who experience similar stressors.

Objectives

The objectives of this activity are to:

1. introduce the concept of stress reactivity,

2. demonstrate blood pressure and heart rate response to one mental stressor and two physical stressors, and

3. facilitate discussion on individual variability in the stress response

Materials required

Automated blood pressure cuff or finger-style blood pressure meter with pulse rate readout ($65-$130: Low cost alternative: manually read pulse rate only). Hand dynamometer ($165-$250: Low cost alternative: make a fist). Directions for mental arithmetic task. Optional: Subjective Units of Distress Scale (SUDS). *See attached figure.*

Time

45-60 minutes (can be adapted for shorter periods of time)

Demonstration

Obtain volunteer(s) to participate in demonstration. Apply blood pressure cuff to left arm and obtain 1-3 resting blood pressure and pulse rate measurements. Participant should be seated comfortably (legs uncrossed) for at least five minutes, with left arm resting on table at heart level. (Low-cost alternative: obtain several manual pulse rate measurements.) Assess perceived level of stress with SUDS or by asking, "How do you feel?"

Discussion   What psychological factors might influence blood pressure and/or pulse rate in this setting? Examples: anxiety over performance in front of peers, desire to please instructor, etc.

Assessment

Reactivity Assessment employing 1-3 stressors. *See attached directions for each task..* Upon completion of each task, assess perceived level of stress as above.

Discussion   What can influence response to each type of stressor? Examples: perception of task as stressful (or not); tendency to enjoy working with numbers (or not); desire to do well; personality traits; perceived level of control; whether psychological factors can influence response to the physical stressors and vice versa; variability of response to the different types of stressors; variability of response between individuals (if more than one volunteer assessed); factors contributing to blood pressure control under these circumstances; etc.

Assignment

Have students write a paragraph assessing their tendency to be a hot reactor and give at least one example in support of their assessment.

Directions for Stress Reactivity Tasks

General Directions: Assess blood pressure and/or pulse rate 2- 3 times during each task. Wait at least 1 minute between each blood pressure assessment. If only pulse rate is being assessed, several 15 or 30 second counts can be taken without any break.

Mental Arithmetic Task Protocol

Read the following directions to the volunteer:
"I would like you to do some calculations. This task consists of starting with one large number and continuously subtracting another smaller, constant number from it. Each time that you mentally subtract the constant number, say your answer out loud. For example, if I asked you

to start at 300 and continuously subtract 7, you would say 300 - 293 - 286 - 279 - 272 - and so one. You should be able to say your answers at the same speed that I just demonstrated. I will correct you if you make a mistake and tell you your last correct answer. You will have five minutes to complete this task. After you start the calculations I will measure your blood pressure and pulse rate 2-3 times. This should not hurt, so try to concentrate on the calculations so that you can perform them as quickly and accurately as possible. OK, when I ask you to begin, start with 1079 and continuously subtract 13 as fast as you can. Begin."

NOTES: Other combinations of numbers may be used, but create a list of the correct answers to refer to during the task. If desired, directions may be taped. To increase stress, set up a competition (use a different number combination) with a student who is not having their blood pressure monitored.

Physical Stress Tasks

Isometric Handgrip Task: Using a hand dynamometer measure maximum strength in the right hand/arm. Following a brief rest, the volunteer maintains a grip on the dynairnometer at 25-30% of maximum while blood pressure and/or pulse rate are assessed 2-3 times. (Low-cost alternative: have volunteer make a fist with the right hand and maintain the pressure while blood pressure and pulse rate are assessed 2-3 times.)

Aerobic Exercise   Have participant run in place for 5 minutes. Measure blood pressure and/or pulse rate 2-3 times immediately following the exercise.

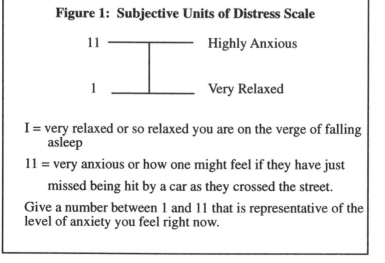

Figure 1: Subjective Units of Distress Scale

11 ——————⊤—————— Highly Anxious

1 _____⊥_____ Very Relaxed

I = very relaxed or so relaxed you are on the verge of falling asleep

11 = very anxious or how one might feel if they have just

missed being hit by a car as they crossed the street.

Give a number between 1 and 11 that is representative of the level of anxiety you feel right now.

39

My Aunt Mattie
Submitted by Ladona Tornabene, Ph.D., CHES
University of South Dakota, Vermillion, SD

Health is a multidimensional concept, yet it is often viewed in only one dimension: the physical. To help illustrate its multidimensional components, the following activity was developed.

Objectives

Students will participate in an activity designed to increase their awareness of the mental, social, emotional, spiritual and physical dimensions of health.

Materials Needed

Chalk and large chalkboard.

Time Needed

Approximately 10 to 20 minutes depending on class size

Description of Activity

This works best on the first or second day of a personal health class. The Instructor begins the lecture by saying, "I need your undivided attention for this part of the lecture. Please, all eyes on me (give a few seconds for students to focus). Then start walking toward the overhead projector (to catch the studentsoff guard) and right before turning it on, say, "Oh, wait a minute! Did I tell you all about my Aunt Mattie?" Obviously everyone will shake their heads saying no. The Instructor can say something like, "Sorry, I teach another class and sometimes can't remember if I've shared it. Anyway, my Aunt Mattie is UNHEALTHY. She —— STOP EVERYBODY!!! I want you to write down exactly what you were thinking when I told you that my Aunt Mattie was unhealthy." Give them a few seconds to write it on a scratch sheet of paper. Then ask for five volunteers to come up to the chalkboard. Ask each to write one of the five dimensions of health as the instructor calls them out (social, emotional, spiritual, mental and physical —leave plenty of space by this one!). Ask each volunteer to keep tabs by placing a mark on the board under that dimension when instructed to do so. Then begin calling on students at random to see what they wrote. All students may be called upon if class size permits. Each time a student reads what was written (i.e. "She had cancer."), ask the class to decide which dimension this should go under and instruct the volunteer standing by that dimension to place a mark on the board under that category (marks can be grouped in fives to make counting easier). This gets challenging when the categories are not as easy to define as when someone writes, "She was depressed." The instructor can then use this opportunity to talk about how these dimensions overlap. Upon completion of this activity, total all marks under each dimension. The class now has a visual representation of their view of health and the instructor can now elaborate on how important ALL the dimensions are to one's health. This activity can also serve as a lead-in to the Health-illness Continuum (Greenberg, 1995).

Evaluation

Throughout the semester, not only on tests, but during lecture and other class assignments, continue to jog students' memories asking them what the five dimensions of health are. This can be effectively woven into the behavior management program by challenging students to go beyond the physical in behavior change and remind them that the WHOLE person is affected to some degree regardless of what dimension they are primarily operating in.

Reference: *Greenberg, J.S. (1995).* Health Education (3rd ed), *Madison, WI: Brown and Benchmark.*

40

Get The Facts From Someone Who Knows

Submitted by John S. Carter, Ph.D.,
The Citadel, Charleston, SC

Audiovisual aids are good when teaching about human sexuality,
however young people are powerfully affected when the message about
safe sex comes from real people with the disease or who have been
infected.

Lesson Objectives

Upon completion of this lesson the student should be able to:

1. appreciate that real people just like him/her get STDs/HIV/
   AIDS;

2. accept the reality that with unprotected or risky sexual behaviors
   come serious (often deadly) consequences;

3. disprove some of the many myths surrounding STDs/HIV/AIDS
   (ie. Yes, it CAN happen to anyone; NO, people with STDs/HIV/
   AIDS DON'T always look dirty, sick, or like they deserve it);
   and

4. enhance written and oral communication skills.

Materials Required

The assignment is to write a 1-2 page paper about what each student
learned from listening to another person speak honestly about their
experiences with STDs/HIV/AIDS. Comments should include what each
student can do differently in their life to minimize risks for acquiring
STDs/HIV/AIDS.

Time Allocations

This project should be assigned no less than two weeks prior to the due
date.

How to Present the Lesson

Teachers can contact the local public health office, hospital or medical
center, or AIDS/HIV foundation regarding a "speakers' bureau." Inquire
as to whether a victim of STDs/AIDS/HIV would be willing to come and

speak to class(es) about how they acquired the disease, life-style behaviors that put them at risk, treatments they've undergone, as well as discuss how uninfected persons can reduce risks of disease acquisition and transmission. Allow for adequate questions and answers during speaker visits.

Organization of Class

The teacher may or may not need to prepare the class beforehand. An atmosphere of mutual respect must be maintained for learning to occur. Encourage anonymous questions to be submitted beforehand; get questions to the speaker for advance preparation.

Variations for different populations

When possible, the ages, gender, racial, and socioeconomic characteristics of the speakers and students should be considered in order to maximize the impact of the message.

Evaluation Techniques

In addition to grading student papers for content and mechanics, a pre- and post-visit examination or survey can be administered to measure student changes in knowledge, attitudes, and behaviors concerning the topics of STDs, HIV, and AIDS.

41

Pyramid Power

Submitted by Roy Wohl, Ph.D., CHES
Washburn University, Topeka, KS

Nutrition education is an important factor in maintenance of lifetime health and well being. Generally, however, college students have quite hectic schedules which leave little time for quality food preparation, thus they tend to exist on fast foods and/or foods of low nutrient density. This lesson focuses on increasing knowledge and awareness of quality nutrition, using the Food Guide Pyramid as a guideline.

Objectives

By the end of this lesson the student should be able to:

1. demonstrate understanding of the Food Guide Pyramid and recommended number of daily servings within each food group,

2. demonstrate knowledge of common serving sizes, and

3. demonstrate knowledge of general dietary guidelines for good health.

Materials

1. 38 questions on individual index cards. Each question should be related to a specific category of the Food Guide Pyramid.

2. Blackboard or a large poster to represent the Food Guide Pyramid for scoring purposes.

3. 10 index cards (each cut in half to make 20) to be used in determining order in which students will answer questions.

4. Hat or box from which to draw index cards.

Time

This lesson is designed to be completed in one 50-minute class period.

Description of Activity

This is for teaching a class of 20 students. Classes with more than 20 students can be further divided, if necessary, to accommodate the lesson. The format is similar to College Bowl, in that each team answers a specific number of questions, with the difference being that a round can end before all questions have been asked if the allotted number of incorrect responses have been given. Questions should be based on lecture information and any other readings for which the students are responsible.

Divide the class in half, either by having students randomly draw their names from the hat or by the instructor composing teams of apparently equal strength prior to class. Ask each team to come up with a name that will strike "nutritional fear" into their opponents. Each team should be seated together in one long row, side-by-side, with each member facing a member of the opposing team, leaving about three feet in between the teams. Once teams are situated, assign the first person in each row the letter "A", the second person "B", etc. until each team member has a letter. Put these same letters on index cards and place them in the hat.

To determine which team will go first, the instructor can draw a letter from the hat for each team. The team with the lower letter in the alphabet will go first (Team #1). Give the hat to the first person in the row on the other team (Team #2). The contest begins with the first person in the row on Team #2 picking a letter out of the hat to designate which opponent on Team #1 will be asked the question. Once a letter is drawn it is not returned to the hat. The hat is then passed to the first person on Team #1 to pick which opponent on Team #2 answers the next question, and continues back and forth down each row until all letters have been drawn. All letters are then returned to the hat and the contest continues for one more round until all questions have been answered or a team has been disqualified for too many incorrect answers.

The instructor should ask the questions, so there is no possible advantage gained by either side from poorly read questions. It is best to read each question only once, slowly, and allow a maximum of 10 seconds for a response. Receiving any assistance from a team member carries a penalty of one fat serving.

Each team has the potential to answer 19 questions (15 servings and 4 fat penalties), in the following breakdown: Grains, etc.,: 6; Fruits: 3-1 ; Vegetables, 4; Milk, etc.,: 3-1; and Meat, etc.,: 3. = 19. The 19 questions represent the total minimum number of servings for all food pyramid categories (15), plus total possible wrong answers (4 fat servings) allowed before disqualification. These four questions are added by including one extra question from each category except Grains. A total of 38 different questions must be prepared. It may also be helpful to have an extra question or two in case an answer is read by mistake. It has happened.

A correct answer gains the team a "serving" in the food pyramid category from which the question originated. An incorrect answer gains the team a "fat" serving - a team is disqualified upon receiving their 5th fat serving. As there are the same number of questions per category as there are servings, once a team has gained all possible servings in a specific category they are forced to try and complete their round using the other categories. If a team has completed a category and the extra question in that same category is selected, it should be moved to the bottom of the pile and used, if necessary, to complete the 19 question set at the end of the round. The team answering the most correct answers is the winner.

If the game is tied, a sudden death playoff can be arranged. The instructor can ask a question of each team and the winner will be the team that answers correctly. If both answer correctly, the format continues until one team has answered incorrectly. Or, declare both teams the winner! Appropriate prizes can be determined, such as: a couple of extra points on the next test for each member of the winning team , 1 sour grapes for the losing team, food/drink discount coupons from the Student Union or local merchants for each team.

Evaluation

Students have found this to be a good learning experience. The format fosters competition and forces students to think quickly, yet is done in a good-natured manner with an overall team concept so students that respond incorrectly are not embarrassed. At the end of the contest, the instructor can review all questions answered incorrectly, entertain questions from students, or use comments to spark a nutrition discussion. The results of the contest also provide the instructor with insight into areas in which further clarification of nutrition concepts may be necessary.

Some Sample Questions

For a Grains, etc., serving:

Q: Which has more protein?
  a. 1 slice whole wheat bread
  b. 1/2 cup lasagna noodles
  c. 1 baked potato
  d. 1/2 cup brown rice

A: 1/2 cup lasagna noodles

For a Grains, etc., serving:
Q: Name one of the two functions of dietary fiber?
A: decrease colo-rectal cancer or remove cholesterol

For a Grains, etc., serving:

Q: How many calories have been eaten in a meal with the followin breakdown, 4 grams fat, 3 grams protein and 2 grams carbohydrate.

A: 56 calories

For a Grains, etc., serving:

Q: Which would be a better choice to eat, a slice of vitamin enriched bread or a slice of whole wheat bread?

A: whole wheat bread

For a Grains, etc., serving:

Q: Which of the following is NOT a standard serving size?
    a. one slice of bread
    b. 1/2 cup cooked spaghetti
    c. 1/4 pound hamburger
    d. 8 ounces of milk

For a Fruit serving:

Q: Which of the following is highest in potassium?
    a. apple
    b. banana
    c. pear
    d. orange

A: banana

For a Fruit serving:

Q: According to the Food Guide Pyramid, what is the recommended range of daily servings of fruit?

A: 2 -4 servings

For a Fruit serving:

Q: What is a standard serving size of orange juice?

A. 6 ounces

For a Fruit serving:

Q: Why did adding fruit to their diet help eliminate the condition known as "scurvy" in the English sailors?

A: Fruit has Vitamin C and they were not getting enough of it.

For a Meat, Beans, etc., serving:
Q: How much does a serving size of meat weigh?
    a.   2 oz.
    b.   3 oz.
    c.   4 oz.
    d.   6 oz.
A: 3 oz.

For a Meat, Beans, etc., serving:
Q: Which of the following is a complete protein?
    a.   hamburger
    b.   kidney bean
    c.   brown rice
    d.   spaghetti noodle
A: hamburger

For a Meat, Beans, etc., serving:
Q: The typical American diet today has about what percentage of calories coming from fat?
    a.   25%
    b.   30%
    c.   37%
    d.   45%
A: 37%

For a Meat, Beans, etc., serving:
Q: Which one is the "gold standard" of protein?
    a.   chicken breast
    b.   meatball
    c.   pork chop
    d.   egg
A: egg

For a Meat, Beans, etc., serving:
Q: Which has more cholesterol, chicken or pasta?
A: chicken

For a Milk, Yogurt, etc., serving:
Q: What percentage of fat is in whole milk?
    a.   1 0%
    b.   25%
    c.   50%
    d.   75%
A: 50%

For a Milk, Yogurt, etc., serving:
Q: Osteoporosis is enhanced by lack of which mineral in the diet?
A: calcium

For a Milk, Yogurt, etc., serving:
Q: Which of the following cheeses is lowest in fat?
    a.   cheddar
    b.   mozzarella
    c.   swiss
    d.   monterey jack
A: mozzarella

For a Milk, Yogurt, etc., serving:
Q: According to the Food Guide Pyramid, what is the recommended range of daily servings of the milk, yogurt and cheese group?
A: 2 -3 servings

For a Vegetable serving:
Q: Which is highest in monounsaturated fat content?
    a.   corn oil
    b.   olive oil
    c.   canola oil
    d.   safflower oil
A. olive oil

For a Vegetable serving:
Q: Which of the following is highest in Vitamin C?
    a.   sweet potato
    b.   green pepper
    c.   mushroom
    d.   broccoli
A: green pepper

For a Vegetable serving:
Q: According to the Food Pyramid, what is the daily recommended range of vegetable servings?
A: 3 - 5 servings

For a Vegetable serving:
Q: Which would provide the most vitamins and minerals.
    a.   canned corn
    b.   steamed frozen corn kernels
    c.   corn on the cob
A: corn on the cob

Digestive System Lineup

Submitted by Suzanne E. Teall, Ph.D.
Montana State University, Bozeman, MT

To fully comprehend human nutrition, students need a basic understanding of the anatomy and physiology of the digestive system and an understanding of the common diseases and disorders that can affect the system.

Objectives

1. Learners will be able to outline the route food takes through the digestive system.

2. Learners will be able to describe the function of digestive system segments and accessory organs.

3. Learners will be able to identify and explain causes, symptoms, and treatments of common diseases and disorders of the digestive system.

Material

5 x 7 index cards with names of digestive system segments, accessory organs, common diseases and disorders and one card with the name of a food.

Examples of cards: incisors, cuspids, bicuspids/tricuspids , salivary glands/saliva, pharynx, esophagus, fundus, body of stomach, pylorus, gastric glands, duodenum, jejunum, ileum, intestinal gland, liver/bile, cecum, gallbladder, pancreas/pancreatic juice, colon, caries, mouth cancer, pancreatitis, pancreatic cancer, diarrhea, constipation, diverticulitis, colitis, appendicitis, gastroenteritis, ulcers, hepatitis, cirrhosis.

Time Needed

1 5 minutes of one class period and two 50-75 minute class periods.

Activity

15 minute time period: Give each student a 5 x 7 index card with the name of a digestive system segment, accessory organ, disease or disorder (listed above). Instruct students to research their card topic and be prepared to talk for 1-3 minutes on the topic at a later assigned class

period. Students with digestive system segments and accessory organ cards are responsible for knowing the function of the system or organ in the digestive process; students with disease and disorder cards are responsible for knowing causes, symptoms, treatment, and how their topic affects digestion and nutrition; and the student with the food card is responsible for knowing the terminology for the food as it travels through the digestive system. Give students one week to do the research.

Session 1:   Clear a large space in the classroom. Instruct the students who have system segments and organ cards to line themselves up, standing, in the order of the digestive process. For this session, begin with incisors and end with pylorus. The disease/disorder people remain seated. Allow 10-15 minutes for the students to arrange themselves. Make sure students are in the correct order. The person who is representing the food stands at the beginning of the line. Beginning with incisors and continuing through the digestive process, each student describes their function in the digestive process and how they affect the food that is eaten. The students with diseases and disorder cards stand and approach the students with the affected segment or organ when that segment or organ is being discussed (e.g. when the students with teeth cards are discussing their topic, the student with the caries card comes forward). The students representing the diseases/disorders present their information and may ask the person representing the affected segment or organ to go back to their seat if the disease/disorder stops that segment or organ from functioning (e.g. dental caries may cause tooth loss, therefore the people representing the teeth may be asked to sit down). The person representing the food travels along the digestive system, holding up cards that indicate the correct name for the food at each stage in the digestive process (e.g. bolus, chyme).

Session 2:   Begin with duodenum and end with anal canal, repeating structure of the first day.

Variations

This activity can be varied depending on class size, depth of instruction, and available time. This activity was designed for a class size of 45 students. If the class is larger, more terms can be used. If the class is smaller, terms can be combined (e.g. have one student cover incisors, cuspids, bicuspids/tricuspids instead of three students). Adjustments can be made in the depth students provide for their individual terms. If less time is available, students can be assigned to describe their term in 30 seconds. If more time is available, students can describe their term in 4-5 minutes.

Evaluation

Evaluation can take the form of exam or quiz questions covering the digestive system segments, organs, and diseases/disorders.

NOTES

NOTES

NOTES

NOTES

NOTES

NOTES

NOTES

NOTES

NOTES

NOTES